The Practice of Pastoral Care

The Practice of Pastoral Care
A Postmodern Approach

Carrie Doehring

WJK WESTMINSTER
JOHN KNOX PRESS
LOUISVILLE • KENTUCKY

Book design by Drew Stevens
Cover design by Pam Poll Graphic Design
Cover art courtesy of Diana Ong / SuperStock

First edition
Published by Westminster John Knox Press
Louisville, Kentucky

This book is printed on acid-free paper that meets the American National Standards Institute Z39.48 standard. ∞

PRINTED IN THE UNITED STATES OF AMERICA

08 09 10 11 12 13 14 15—10 9 8 7 6 5 4

Library of Congress Cataloging-in-Publication Data is on file at the Library of Congress, Washington, D.C.

ISBN-13: 978-0-664-22684-8
ISBN-10: 0-664-22684-1

For George

Ubi caritas et amor, Deus ibi est.
Where charity and love are, there is God.

(ninth-century Latin chant, based on 1 John 4:16, traditionally sung during the footwashing that is part of the Maundy Thursday service)

Contents

Acknowledgments

I am indebted to many colleagues for conversations about postmodern approaches to pastoral care: my colleagues in Boston University's PhD program in Counseling Psychology and Religion, notably Edouard Fontenot, who carefully read drafts and engaged in conversations about Neville's theology; my colleagues at Boston University's School of Theology; colleagues in the Society for Pastoral Theology, who read previous drafts (Nancy Ramsay, James Poling, John Patton, Charles Scalise, Ulrike Guthrie); my colleagues at Iliff School of Theology, namely Larry Kent Graham, Tom Troeger, Dana Wilbanks, and Don Rickard; and finally, students who used drafts of the manuscript as a course text at Boston University School of Theology and Iliff School of Theology, Denver. Stephanie Egnotovich, senior editor at Westminster John Knox, was enormously helpful in revising the manuscript and helping me present my ideas clearly.

My deepest gratitude is extended to my husband, George Magnuson, to whom this book is dedicated, who continually forms and reforms with me a marriage and family based on promises of faithfulness rooted in God's covenant with creation. I also want to acknowledge with deep thanks all those who are part of this web of family life—my sons, Jordan and Alex; my mother and father; George's children and their spouses, Colette and Kelly, Renee and Peter, Chad and Beth, Blake and Colette, Kendall and Stephanie; and my brothers and sisters, Nancy, Carl, Laura, and Peter.

Introduction

Robert Johnson,[1] an African American Baptist minister, enters the Woodside Nursing Home with a heavy heart, for he has some sad news for a resident, Emily Watson. Her oldest son has been killed in an automobile accident. The minister has prayed for the knowledge and wisdom he will need to assess Mrs. Watson's most immediate psychological and spiritual needs, so that he can work with the nursing home staff to provide care as she experiences acute grief. His care will include planning and conducting a funeral service for her son, and then being present with Mrs. Watson over the coming months as she grieves this death.

I have written this book for those, like Robert Johnson, who have been called to a particular religious vocation—the ministry of pastoral care—in a historical context when many long-standing assumptions about truth are being questioned and critically appraised (Lartey 2002, 1). In such a context, pastoral caregivers like Robert Johnson face the challenge of keeping "alive in the post-modern world a religious vision created in a distinctly premodern cultural context, honed to a level of sophistication and lived out courageously through many centuries of premodernity" (Lakeland 1997, 39). What sort of religiously based care can be offered by those who use a postmodern approach to knowledge and assume that knowledge about humanity, the world, and

---

1. All of the case studies are fictional.

ıt is named as God is socially constructed in the midst of complex
orical contexts?

n my approach to pastoral care I invite pastoral caregivers to view
r ministry through trifocal lenses that include premodern, mod-
and postmodern approaches to knowledge.[2] Using a *premodern*
pastors assume for the moment that God or that which is sacred
be glimpsed and apprehended to some degree through sacred
, religious rituals and traditions, and religious and spiritual expe-
es—the way transcendent realities seemed to be known within
ancient and medieval church prior to the use of critical
)aches to knowledge introduced by Enlightenment thinkers.
Using a *modern* lens, pastoral caregivers draw upon rational and
empirical methods, like biblical critical methods, medical knowledge,
and the social sciences, in offering pastoral care. A *postmodern* lens
brings into focus the contextual and provisional nature of knowledge,
including knowledge of God.[3]

Pastoral caregivers who draw upon all three approaches to knowledge
can use a premodern lens to focus on the careseeker's religious and spiritual experiences of feeling connected to God or the sacred. They can
explore when and how careseekers experience this connection, and
whether spiritual and religious practices induce a sense of God's presence
in their lives. Do such moments come in the midst of worship, during
the singing of a hymn, through participation in a sacrament or ritual, or
in the contemplation of an icon or statue in the sanctuary of their community of faith? Do they experience a sense of the sacred in the beauty
of nature or the arts, or in the daily ritual of prayer? Since the purpose of
religious and spiritual practices is to mediate experiences of the sacred or
divine, pastoral caregivers can use a premodern lens to focus on such
practices as if direct apprehensions of the divine are possible.

Using a premodern lens, Mr. Johnson can be aware of moments in
his conversation with Mrs. Watson when it seems as though she is able
to connect with God. Such moments might come when they pray
together or when Mrs. Watson expresses her fears about her son's suffering as he died. In looking ahead at the next several days, Mr. Johnson can explore with Mrs. Watson what spiritual practices might help
her feel connected to God in the midst of her anguish over the death of

---

2. As Lartey (2003, 2) says, "It is . . . important to note that all of these conditions [of premodernity, modernity, and postmodernity] exist to different degrees all over the globe and that they do so simultaneously."

3. In this text I use the term postmodern to refer to a social constructionist approach to knowledge. I do not use the term to describe a cultural state, as is often done (Lakeland 1997, ix; Couture 2003, 85).

her son. What has helped her cope with past experiences of suffering? If she has found meaning in reading from the book of Psalms, then she and Mr. Johnson can turn to these psalms as they sit together. Perhaps particular hymns or religious music that have offered comfort in the past can be a resource now. Using a premodern lens, Mr. Johnson can focus on whether and how Mrs. Watson is experiencing a connection with God.

Mr. Johnson can shift to using a modern approach to knowledge during his pastoral care conversation when he draws upon biblical critical methods, systematic modern theological perspectives, and psychological and medical perspectives on death and grief. His knowledge of how biblical critical methods have been used to explore the many meanings of the psalms can be relevant if Mrs. Watson finds comfort and meaning in the psalms. His familiarity with several theological perspectives on God's presence in the midst of suffering offers him a range of ways to respond to Mrs. Watson's anguish over her son's suffering as he died. His knowledge about shock and acute stress can make him aware of how Mrs. Watson is responding psychologically to the news of her son's death. In drawing upon knowledge gained from modern approaches to understanding biblical texts, theological problems like suffering, and the psychological experience of acute stress, Mr. Johnson uses a modern lens.

Mr. Johnson shifts to using a postmodern lens during the conversation when he is aware of how much Mrs. Watson's response to this crisis is shaped in myriad ways by her unique history and various aspects of her social identity like her gender, race, religion, social class, sexual orientation, and age. He wonders what unique experiences as an African American woman of faith she will bring to grieving the sudden death of her son. In ongoing pastoral care conversations, he can draw upon her religious practices and language to engage in a process of coconstructing religious ways of connecting with the sacred and making sense of this death. His sermon, written specifically for this occasion, will reflect the contextual psychological, cultural, and theological meanings he has constructed with Mrs. Watson. A postmodern lens will help him focus on the particular religious meanings and ways of connecting with God that they coconstruct, which are relevant to her in the immediate crisis and long-term process of understanding this death.

Movement among premodern, modern, and postmodern approaches to knowledge in pastoral care often follows a pattern in which pastoral caregivers begin with a premodern approach, in order to help careseekers gain a sense of the sacred or connection with God in acute moments of crisis. Pastoral caregivers also initially rely upon modern approaches to understand medical or psychological aspects of a crisis. While they are using premodern approaches to connect with God, and modern approaches to understand what has happened, they may realize how much they do not and cannot know, and how their experience is shaped by who they are and the context in which they live. With this realization comes an acknowledgment of the provisionality of knowledge and an awareness of the relevance of a postmodern approach.

Pastoral caregivers who are able to use trifocal lenses are less likely to limit their care by only using a premodern, modern, or postmodern approach to knowledge. An exclusive use of premodern approaches to care is evident in a form of pastoral care called biblical or nouthetic counseling, in which biblical texts are literally interpreted and used in directive ways.[4] Pastoral caregivers who only use premodern approaches to knowledge, bracketing the critical approaches of modern and postmodern thinkers, believe the absolute truth of their religious traditions, similar to the beliefs of the church in ancient and medieval times. In an extreme form of premodern pastoral care, caregivers reject scientific knowledge altogether.[5] Less extreme are the nostalgic premodern approaches to knowledge (Lakeland 1997, 17), in which pastoral caregivers use religious sources, such as sacred texts, doctrine, ecclesial statements, and spiritual/mystical experiences, as though they are direct revelations of what they name as God, and not interpretations of religious experiences and constructions of theological knowledge. Such caregivers, for example, might reference biblical texts in reflecting upon care without ever using the biblical critical methods with which they are familiar. Or they may believe that what they name as God is directly revealed to them, unmediated by human interpretation.[6]

If the minister in the opening illustration, Robert Johnson, used such an approach, he would probably see no need to draw upon any psychological understandings of grief or consult with the nursing home staff about how Mrs. Watson was coping psychologically with the news of her son's death. He could, for example, direct Mrs. Watson to rejoice

4. The National Association of Nouthetic Counselors (NANC) was organized in the 1970s and based upon the writings of Jay Adams (1970). This organization adopted the term "nouthetic" from the Greek word "nouthesis" used in the epistles of the New Testament. They use literal norms to interpret biblical texts in order to instruct, admonish, warn, and correct Christians in crisis.

5. "The fundamentalist reassertion of a premodern vision [is] secure in the conviction that modernity, and what has followed is the work of Satan, to be eradicated" (Lakeland 1997, 35).

6. Such was the experience of some Christians who viewed Mel Gibson's film *The Passion of the Christ* as a direct revelation of Jesus' suffering. *New York Times* film critic A. O. Scott notes this distinction: "I take 'The Passion of the Christ' to be an interpretation of Scripture, while some of my readers take it as very close to Scripture itself" (Scott 2004, 21).

over her son's entry into heaven. If her son did not met her minister's criteria for salvation, Mrs. Watson would be directed to celebrate her own salvation and acknowledge this final separation from her son. Depending upon Mrs. Watson's own way of being in the world during this time of acute grief, she might find this mode of care either comforting or disturbing.

Pastoral caregivers who draw exclusively upon modern approaches to knowledge are liable to miss contextual meanings that are not part of their theoretical perspectives. Relying on modern biblical critical methods—form, tradition history, redaction, source, and several other methods—they may assume that questions about the meaning of a text can be answered conclusively, and that such meanings can be applied in any pastoral care conversation. Mr. Johnson, for example, may develop ideas about the meaning of the resurrection by engaging in biblical critical studies, and he may endeavor to make these ideas fit into all of his pastoral care conversations and sermon preparations, whether or not they are relevant to the particular circumstances of the death of Mrs. Watson's son. Or he might rely exclusively on a theory about grief and use it to label all of Mrs. Watson's responses to her son's death. Any aspect of her grief or theology not seen through the lens of his psychological and theological perspectives will likely go unnoticed.

Pastoral caregivers who draw exclusively on a postmodern approach to knowledge run the risk of neglecting careseekers in crisis who need to experience a tangible connection with God that seems immediate and direct. Pastoral caregivers aware of postmodern questions about whether and how people can apprehend a sense of the sacred may become inhibited in conversations with careseekers about spiritual and religious ways of coping with stress. Their fear of knowing how to respond when careseekers describe seemingly simplistic or naive ways of understanding God may make it hard for caregivers to have any conversations about God or the careseeker's sense of the sacred. Pastoral caregivers may be overly aware of the complexities opened up when postmodern perspectives are used. In addition, a postmodern approach in which the pastoral caregiver simply generates more and more ways of understanding who God is—indeed, endless possibilities—without focusing on meanings that are relevant and pragmatically useful can leave people in crisis without any immediate spiritual comfort or guidance.

In using a trifocal lens to shift among premodern, modern, and postmodern approaches to knowledge, pastoral caregivers draw upon all of the historical and contemporary resources of their religious, intellectual, and cultural traditions. Their premodern lens gives them access to the long and rich history of religious traditions in ancient and medieval historical periods. Using a modern lens, they draw upon the vast knowledge generated by rational and scientific methods, notably biblical critical methods, systematic modern theologies, and medical and social scientific theories about human experience. A postmodern lens brings into focus the contextual, provisional nature of knowledge and how knowledge is socially constructed, particularly through systems of power and privilege.

In the pages that follow, I will describe one way of envisioning pastoral care that makes use of trifocal lenses. Having introduced the approach to care described in this book, I will continue with some definitions of basic terms. Throughout the history of Christianity the term "pastoral care" has described care offered by representatives of this religious tradition. The adjective "pastoral" refers to the image of shepherd found in Hebrew and Christian Scriptures and traditions. The shepherd's care of the flock has been used extensively as an image that describes how Jewish and Christian leaders care for members of their religious communities. While not all pastoral caregivers are ordained,[7] they are all accountable to religious organizations and communities of faith for the care they offer. For example, Robert Johnson is accountable to his congregation and to his denomination (including its code of ethics) for the care he offers as a representative of his religious tradition.

One difficulty with the term "pastoral care" is that it refers to Christian and Jewish religious traditions and cannot be used to describe the care offered by Buddhist, Muslim, or Hindu caregivers. Institutional chaplain's departments and organizations that certify chaplains have started to use the term "spiritual care" to describe caregivers attending to the spiritual dimensions of persons. This term can too easily refer to individualistic spirituality that lacks any connection with communities of faith and religious traditions in which spirituality has been historically rooted. Individualistic spirituality may not fully draw upon the rich symbol systems, liturgies, music, and sacred writings that make up a religious tradition. If a chaplain in the nursing home where Mrs. Watson lives offered her individualistic spiritual care, he or she might inadvertently bypass what could be Mrs. Watson's most important spiritual

---

7. If lay members become pastoral caregivers, they are usually given training, supervision, and oversight by their faith community. Shelp and Sunderland (2000) describe a model for training lay caregivers. They have used this model in extensive caregiving programs to people with AIDS or Alzheimer's disease, as well as frail elderly persons and young adults with disabilities or terminal illness.

resource, namely, the prayers, hymns, worship experiences, and beliefs of her Baptist tradition. For example, if Mrs. Watson talked about the homecoming service for her son, a chaplain without knowledge of how she celebrates death in her tradition might make premature judgments about her denial of the final physical separation that death brings.

Pastoral care takes many forms, depending upon the historical and global context in which it is offered.[8] In a North American context, it usually takes the form of crisis intervention in response to a sudden loss or experience of violence, followed by supportive care. Crisis intervention is a form of care offered to persons, families, and communities who because of complicating factors cannot move through a crisis or transition by simply drawing upon their usual support systems and resources. Mrs. Watson, for example, will need crisis intervention because the news of her son's death is unexpected and shocking, and comes at a time when she happens to be coping with the losses that accompany becoming an increasingly frail elderly woman.

When the acute phase of the crisis starts to subside, care becomes more supportive as the careseeker copes with any long-term effects of the crisis. In this book, I describe crisis intervention and the assessments and crisis strategies that need to be done by the caregiver in chapters on assessing risk, loss, violence, and compulsive ways of coping with stress (chapters 4 and 5). The subsequent discussion of systemic factors and theological reflection (chapters 6 and 7) has more relevance to the ongoing supportive ministry that follows crisis intervention. Such care offers a "sustaining presence" (Shelp and Sunderland 2000, 28) to people who have experienced a past crisis and continue to live with chronic stress due to health, relational, or social conditions that are not likely to change. For example, pastoral care offered to people who are frail and elderly is often supportive care that helps to sustain them in the midst of multiple losses. Supportive care for people in chronic experiences of suffering can be informed by sociocultural understandings of the suffering that occurs in contexts of social oppression. Elderly people who lack financial resources may have limited options when it comes to long-term care. In being supportive of frail, elderly persons without financial resources, caregivers can widen their perspectives to include the sociopolitical context and strategies for seeking justice.

8. In their historical review of writings on pastoral care, Clebsch and Jaekle (1964) note that there seem to be as many forms of pastoral care as there are pastoral caregivers. Lartey (2004) describes the many indigenous forms of pastoral care that exist in today's global context.

Pastoral caregivers usually learn about crisis intervention and supportive care through academic courses, field education, and internships. Without further training and accountability to certifying organizations like the American Association of Pastoral Counselors and the Association for Clinical Pastoral Education, they are not equipped to offer other kinds of care, such as pastoral psychotherapy, spiritual direction, and family counseling; providing such care would be unethical. The steps of pastoral care I describe remain within the purview of crisis intervention and supportive care that theologically educated caregivers can offer.

Sources of Authority in Pastoral Care

Many sources of authority are used in providing pastoral care. Sources can be likened to diamonds that lay embedded in the earth. The norms used to interpret them are like the methods used to mine and cut diamonds. One source of authority is religious: the Hebrew Scriptures, the New Testament, liturgy, doctrines, and religious practices, including spiritual practices. Biblical critical methods provide modern norms for interpreting sacred texts. Modern and postmodern theological perspectives provide norms for evaluating and elaborating the interpretation of Scripture, doctrines, and practices. For example, Christian liberation theologies often use the norm of valuing the voices of people who are marginalized in a social system. This norm can be used to reflect theologically on Scripture and religious traditions.

Besides religious sources and norms of authority, pastoral care draws upon narrative sources and norms of authority, in that both the careseeker's and caregiver's stories are valued as creative ways in which persons, families, and cultures construct meaning. The social sciences, particularly psychological studies, help pastoral caregivers examine psychological experiences as sources of authority, interpreting such experiences using a variety of psychological perspectives, like psychodynamic theories of personality, developmental theories, family systems theory, and theories about mental illness, to name a few. Cultural studies have helped pastoral caregivers understand how the social identity of careseekers is shaped by their gender, race, sexual orientation, social class, and religious identities. A variety of theoretical perspectives—feminist and gender studies; gay, lesbian, and transgender studies; African American, Hispanic, Asian American, and other ethically or racially oriented studies—offers norms for interpreting the careseeker's experience of his or her social identity.

A Cross-Disciplinary Contextual Approach

A cross-disciplinary approach, called a critical correlational method, brings these sources and norms of authority into dialogue (Poling and Miller 1985; Browning 1991; Doehring 1999; Ramsay 1998). The postmodern purpose of such cross-disciplinary critical dialogue is not to generate universal knowledge and theories, but to develop contextual understandings of persons in crisis and formulate strategies for seeking their well-being and justice. My approach to pastoral care is highly contextual, reflecting my scholarly, pastoral, and clinical contexts, and will be most relevant to persons whose religious, educational, and professional context are similar to mine. It is not presented as an approach to pastoral care that is universally useful; rather, it is one of a myriad of ways to offer pastoral care.

In order for readers to evaluate whether my approach is relevant, I will briefly describe my context. I am an Anglo-American woman raised as a Roman Catholic in a middle-class home in the United States and later Canada, by parents of a mixed-religious marriage (my father is an agnostic, and my mother is Roman Catholic). I was ordained in the Presbyterian Church in Canada and was the minister in two village churches in Ontario for nine years, before moving to Boston, where I completed a PhD in pastoral psychology at Boston University. I taught there for eleven years and was a psychologist and clinical supervisor at the Danielsen Institute, a pastoral counseling and mental health center affiliated with Boston University. I also was a parttime minister at North Street Congregational Church in Medford, Massachusetts. Currently, I teach at Iliff School of Theology. My concern with offering a pragmatically useful description of pastoral care reflects my pastoral and clinical experiences of providing care that draws upon the richness and complexity of premodern, modern, and postmodern approaches to knowledge, especially religious and theological knowledge.

The Shape of This Book

In this book, I pose questions about how to engage in such care and offer seven steps pastoral caregivers can follow. While for the sake of convenience I describe these steps as if they occur in a linear sequence, in actuality a caregiver moves back and forth among them. It may be more helpful to think of them as seven moments in pastoral care:

1. Listening empathically to the careseeker's story
2. Examining the helpful and unhelpful ways in which one's own story is engaged
3. Establishing the contract of care by reviewing whether there are or may be limits to the confidentiality of the pastoral care conversation, psychological needs that may result in sexual misconduct, conflicting dual roles, limits to the caregiver's expertise, and limits to the caregiver's availability
4. Assessing psychological issues to do with loss, violence, and ways of coping with the resulting stress, and proposing initial strategies for healing
5. Assessing the strengths and liabilities of the careseeker's cultural, community, and family systems, as well as close relationships
6. Reflecting theologically and proposing theological norms
7. Developing strategies for seeking healing and justice

Each of these actions is elaborated in the outline of chapters that follows.

I devote the first three chapters to basic concepts and skills related to listening to both the stories of careseekers and one's own story. In these chapters, I emphasize the "how to" of pastoral care. In chapter 1, I describe the first step—listening to the stories of those seeking care—and some basic ingredients in caregiving relationships: empathy, relational boundaries, and power dynamics. Chapter 1 opens with an example of a pastoral care conversation in the format of a script, which is called a verbatim. In chapter 2, I discuss how to listen to our own stories, as they are evoked by the careseeker's story. The caregiver's story can be in one moment a rich resource and in the next moment a roadblock to providing care. I describe how to monitor the ways in which a pastoral caregiver's own story helps or hinders pastoral care. At the end of this chapter I introduce the first in a series of exercises that come at the end of chapters 2–8. By completing these exercises, readers can follow the steps of pastoral care using their own case studies.

Chapter 3 focuses on good listening practices and provides readers with an opportunity to reexamine their own listening skills. The ways in which pastoral caregivers sit with and listen to people in pain reflect their embedded theologies, that is, the theologies that they put into practice. I show caregivers how to use psychological and spiritual resources as they reflect on aspects of their listening style that may communicate an embedded theology that is at odds with their deliberative theology—the theology in which they believe. This chapter can be especially helpful in supervised experiences in which verbatim, audio, and videotapes of pastoral care conversations are used.

In chapter 4, I consider the contract of care that is implicitly or explicitly established at the outset of pastoral care, and how this contract is based upon ministerial codes of conduct. Such contracts ensure that careseekers will not be harmed. If, in the course of a pastoral care conversation, the caregiver suspects the presence of child or elder abuse, which would cause there to be limits to confidentiality, the potential for sexual boundaries to be crossed in the caregiving relationship, conflicting dual roles, the need for referral or limits to when and how they can be available for urgent pastoral care, then the caregiver must refer to his or her code of conduct, seek consultation, and take appropriate action to safeguard the careseeker's well-being. If, for example, a pastoral caregiver like Robert Johnson were to receive any indication that Mrs. Watson is being sexually or physically abused, he would immediately seek consultation with his denominational legal representatives about whether or not he is legally and morally obliged to report this abuse. I consider the full range of a caregiver's accountability by discussing (1) the limits of confidentiality when caregivers suspect physical, sexual, or emotional abuse or neglect, (2) sexual misconduct, (3) the dual roles of pastoral caregivers, (4) the limits of expertise, and (5) availability for providing urgent care.

Chapters 5 and 6 concern steps four and five, which have to do with the kinds of psychological and systemic assessments that caregivers do as they listen to a careseeker's story. In these two chapters I use the social sciences, cultural studies, and family systems theory as sources and norms of authority. In chapter 5, caregivers consider how to explore the psychological dimensions of the careseeker's story. Careseekers are often dealing with life-cycle transitions and crises that have to do with loss, such as leaving home as young adults, ending a pregnancy, entering a committed relationship, becoming parents, going through a divorce, or becoming unemployed. Or they may be dealing with crises shaped by violence, like experiences of sexual assault and abuse, and partner violence. I provide caregivers with the knowledge and skills they need to assess whether loss and/or violence are themes in careseekers' stories. I also discuss how to assess the ways people cope with stress, especially through the use of compulsive behaviors and addictive substances. I describe the psychological needs of persons dealing with various kinds of loss, violence, and ways of coping, as well as strategies for providing care.

Chapter 6 describes the fifth step: assessing the strengths and weaknesses of cultural, community, and family systems to determine if these systems exacerbate or ameliorate the careseeker's crisis or transition. Here I use cultural studies to describe how to assess the careseeker's social identity, in terms of which aspects of social identity may afford or deny resources to careseekers in their crises. The role of a church community is discussed. The family's past and present involvement in the careseeker's crisis is assessed, using family systems theory. Marital studies are used to assess intimate relationships. Along with descriptions of the liabilities that may be involved in cultural, community, and family systems, I describe strategies for seeking justice. Without cultural, community, and family change, individual healing is often not possible.

In chapter 7, I discuss the value of adding a theological perspective to this cross-cultural dialogue. In this sixth step, caregivers use criteria from a postmodern approach to knowledge to identify theological perspectives that (1) are contextually meaningful in terms of the careseeker's experiences, (2) can be used to engage in cross-disciplinary dialogues, and (3) are pragmatically useful in developing strategies for seeking care and justice. I illustrate how to use these criteria to assess the relevance of two theological perspectives: Neville's theology concerning religious symbols (*The Truth of Broken Symbols*; Neville 1996) and Poling's theology concerning evil (Poling 1996). I conclude by using Neville's and Poling's theological perspectives to arrive at theological norms that can be used as a basis for a plan of care.

In chapter 8, I describe how to engage in the last step of pastoral care: developing a plan. The first goal of such a plan is to attend to the safety of careseekers and help them establish a sense of stability by examining the ways in which careseekers are coping with the acute stress that may be part of experiences of loss and violence. Pastoral caregivers can focus on how persons in crisis use religious and spiritual ways of coping that connect them with God and their communities of faith. As caregivers help careseekers find spiritual and religious ways of experiencing safety and stability, a relationship of trust forms. When the first goal of achieving safety and stability is reached and a trusting relationship is established, the second goal is possible: mourning the losses incurred by the crisis and holding those who caused harm accountable for their actions. The third goal is to reconnect with the ordinary goodness of life.

These three goals are considered first in relation to individual careseekers and their immediate relationships, and then in relation to the community and larger society of which they are a part. Persons living within violent family systems, communities, and societies are not going to be able to achieve safety and a sense of stability until the violent systems in which they live are transformed. In achieving the second goal of mourning losses and holding those who have done harm accountable for their actions, caregivers can work with law enforcement agencies and social services to hold perpetrators of violence accountable. When harm has been caused by compulsive ways of coping with stress, like substance abuse and dependency, caregivers can refer careseekers to 12-step programs that offer effective strategies and support for those taking a moral inventory of the harm caused by their addictions. Given the systemic need to examine not only the healing of individual careseekers, but the healing of family, community, and societal systems, caregivers will collaborate with other professional resource persons to develop plans of care that seek both healing and justice.

I turn in chapter 9 to describing how a minister would move among these seven moments of care in responding to a crisis involving loss, violence, and alcoholism. Using the novel and film *Affliction* as a rich and complex case study, I begin by having the reader imagine being the minister at a family scene in which violence erupts. By stepping into the shoes of the minister portrayed in the novel, I describe ways in which a pastoral caregiver could have responded to the complicated and profound needs of the main character, Wade Whitehouse, and averted the bloodbath of violence that resulted from his needs not being addressed. In this case study, the need for pastoral care is compelling, and the artistic beauty of both the film and the novel draws viewers and readers lyrically into the suffering portrayed in this narrative.

In the conclusion, I draw upon theoretical perspectives in pastoral theology to discuss the relevance and meaningfulness of the contextual postmodern approach to pastoral care used in this book. The purpose of this conclusion is to locate this approach to pastoral care within the liberal Protestant North American tradition of pastoral theology shaped by the last twenty-five years and to describe how this particular approach to care is one way of responding to the challenges of providing pastoral care that acknowledges the social construction of knowledge.

1

Basic Ingredients of Caregiving Relationships

The first step that a caregiver can take in seeking healing and justice for someone who is suffering is simple and natural: the caregiver listens to the careseeker's story. In illustration, we begin with the dialogue between a minister and a woman who comes to him for care.[1]

A Pastoral Care Conversation

The Rev. Sam Lee arranged a meeting with a middle-aged Korean American woman who attended worship at the Korean Methodist Church in Springfield for the first time a few weeks ago. She hadn't talked to anyone, but she had written her name, Mrs. Wood, and phone number in the guest book. As he did with all local visitors, Sam Lee made a follow-up call. During their conversation she asked whether she could come and see him about a family problem. She came to his office on a weekday morning. His office was arranged so that guests sat with their backs to the office door while he directly faced both his guests and the open door. After greetings, Mrs. Wood sat in the offered chair and began to speak of why she had attended worship. Afterwards, Sam Lee tried to recall the conversation, writing

---

1. This conversation has been written in the form of a script, which is called a verbatim. Statements made by the caregiver and careseeker are numbered so that they can be referenced in reflections on the verbatim.

it in the form of a verbatim that he could reflect upon in a peer consultation group. He numbered each response so that he and his colleagues could refer to responses in their discussion.

Mrs. Wood (1): I usually worship with my husband, Tom. We go to First Congregational Church on Main Street. A few weeks ago, I was upset about my mother, and for some strange reason I thought it would be comforting to worship in a Korean congregation. I had heard that this congregation was friendly. That's why I came here.

Rev. Lee (1): I'm glad you came. What was troubling you?

Mrs. Wood (2): My mother stayed with us recently for several weeks. Her visit upset me because she talked about what her life has been like. She's usually reserved and doesn't say much about the past.

Rev. Lee (2): I wonder what made her less reserved.

Mrs. Wood (3): She's getting older now. She's in her late sixties. My father died about a year ago. It's been hard for her to be by herself. I didn't realize this. I thought she'd like being on her own. They didn't have a very good marriage.

Rev. Lee (3): What was their marriage like?

Mrs. Wood (4): My dad wasn't Korean. He met my mother when he was in Korea as an American soldier. I never heard much about how they met. That was something they didn't talk about. There was a lot they didn't talk about. In fact they didn't talk much. It was like the Cold War between them. I thought sometimes that they just hated each other. Mom looked after the house and didn't go out much. It's been hard to get her to travel and visit her kids and grandchildren. We decided that we'd set up the visits and just make her get out of that empty house sometimes.

Rev. Lee (4): Their marriage sounds so sad. Not what God wants for us. (There are a few moments of silence.)

Mrs. Wood (5): If she came here and people knew about her past, they would judge her.

Rev. Lee (5): Judge her for what?

Mrs. Wood (6) (crying): She told me that she met my father when she worked in a bar. She left home when she was fourteen because there wasn't enough food for the family. She became a barmaid, and sometimes went out with the men afterwards. It makes me feel sick to know she was a prostitute.

Rev. Lee (6): It must have been shocking to hear this.

Mrs. Wood (7): I was totally surprised. I've been going over and over in my mind what my mother said. Sometimes I'm shouting at her or at the people who judge her.

Rev. Lee (7): You thought I might judge her.

Mrs. Wood (8): Well, you are a minister. And sin is all about sex. I'm sorry. I'm more American than Korean. My mother never spent any time with other Koreans.

Rev. Lee (8): Women like your mother don't talk about their past because they often feel so ashamed. Among Koreans, it would be hard to hide her past. As soon as people knew she had married an American soldier, they would make assumptions.

Mrs. Wood (9): I realize that now. I never did when I was growing up. I just thought that there was something wrong with her. I feel so stupid that I never suspected anything.

Rev. Lee (9): Your mother protected you. (There is silence for a few moments.)

Mrs. Wood (10): That's a nice way to put it. (More silence.)

Mrs. Wood (11): You know, I was afraid to come to you because you're a Korean minister.

Rev. Lee (11): Yes, people often think that ministers will be judgmental. My children have taught me to not be so judgmental. They have challenged me. I'm a better listener now.

Mrs. Wood (12): I'd like to come back for worship. But it's hard. Some of the older Korean women in the choir look very stern.

Rev. Lee (12): Perhaps we could meet again after you've been to worship.

Mrs. Wood (13): That would be good. Even though I'd like to just ignore what my mother said, I can't.

Rev. Lee (13): Would you like to have a prayer before you leave?

Mrs. Wood (14): I'm sorry, Rev. Lee. I know I should have you say a prayer. I just don't feel comfortable with that right now.

Rev. Lee (14): You are an honest person. That's good. I will see you again, I hope.

Mrs. Wood (15): Thank you so much for your help.

In this dialogue, Mr. Lee is a good listener. He pays attention to what goes on within him, identifying his reactions. Does he feel like giving advice and being in charge? Does he feel like withdrawing? Does he become critical? Is he anxious? He explores his reactions in terms of his own story, especially stressful experiences that have had an impact on him. He has also learned to pay attention to larger cultural stories connected with being a Korean immigrant. In the next chapter, I will describe Mr. Lee's story. But first, we examine concepts concerning what it means to be a good listener.

Empathy and Relational Boundaries

Empathy plays a central role in pastoral care. It is a means of imaginatively stepping into the shoes of another person and seeing the world from her or his perspective. However, at the same time they make this connection, caregivers must maintain their own perspective and be aware of what is happening within both themselves and the caring relationship. Empathy involves two simultaneous and opposite relational skills: (1) making connection with another person by experiencing what it is like to be that person, and (2) maintaining separation from the other person by being aware of one's own feelings and thoughts. Empathy is a balancing act.

In the conversation above, Sam Lee is able to imagine what it is like for both Mrs. Wood and her mother. He puts himself in her mother's shoes when he asks Mrs. Wood why her mother was suddenly less reserved about her past, and what her mother's marriage was like. He expresses sadness about this marriage. As he connects emotionally with Mrs. Wood and her mother, his responses begin to communicate his empathy. He also has some perspective on their experiences, which he indicates when he makes the faith claim that God does not want partners to remain stuck in cold, angry relational dynamics.

One problem in pastoral care is fusion, which occurs when care-givers become too immersed in the careseeker's experience. This kind of fusion, or merger, is common for beginners in pastoral care, especially if caregivers feel that they have many things in common with the care-seeker. Overidentifying with a careseeker can make it difficult for a caregiver to be aware of her own feelings and at the same time monitor what is happening in the relationship. She may as a result become over-involved in helping careseekers.

In this dialogue Sam Lee could have become overinvolved with Mrs. Wood at any point in the conversation. For example, when she says that sin is all about sex, and that she is more American than Korean, Sam Lee might have felt compelled to assure her that many ministers, him-self included, do not equate sex with sin. He might have preached about sexual intimacy as sacred. Or he could have urged Mrs. Wood to make this congregation her Korean home, a place where she could explore her ethnic identity. However, in responding in these ways, he would have taken over the conversation with his agenda. He would have missed the cues that Mrs. Wood had just given, that she needed to maintain her distance from him and this congregation because of her ambivalence toward her mother.

At the opposite extreme, some caregivers distance themselves emo-tionally from the careseeker. If this had happened with Sam Lee, he might have responded defensively to Mrs. Wood's remarks about sex as sin and her being more American than Korean by saying, "Well, why did you come here in the first place, and why did you come to speak with me?" This response would protect him from her anger, but if he were to feel that he is the target of her anger, he would miss the cue that she is angry with herself and her mother. Sam Lee doesn't make this mistake. He is able to separate himself from the dynamics going on within Mrs. Wood, and he connects with Mrs. Wood's mother's expe-rience of shame about her past.

Merger, empathy, and disengagement lie on a continuum. Empathy is in the middle, and involves both being separate from and connected with the other person. Anxiety or stress can lead a caregiver either to become too separated from the other person and disengaged emotion-ally or to become too connected or fused with the other, such that the caregiver can't distinguish his or her own feelings from the feelings of the person seeking care. Various family and communal experiences (like being part of a community of faith) can create tendencies toward greater disconnection or fusion with those seeking care. For example, what if Sam Lee had felt responsible as a child for his mother's well-being in his family of origin, and didn't recognize how this dynamic recurred in his adult relationships with women in distress? He might have become overinvolved in his conversation with Mrs. Wood, wanting her to dispel her feelings of sadness and anger before she left his office. The other extreme could also occur, if Sam had felt helpless and angry about his childhood experience of his mother's distress. He might have distanced himself from Mrs. Wood, telling himself that he could not help her because she was too confused and angry.

Empathy is important to pastoral caregivers and practical theologians because it describes both the psychological and religious dynamics of relationships. Many pastoral theologians (Karaban 1991; McCarthy 1992; Schlauch 1990, 1995) have used the human dynamics of empathy to describe the divine dynamics of a transcendent being entering into human suffering. Indeed, the Christian symbol of resurrection is about God entering into human life, suffering, and overcoming the destruction that can be part of terrible suffering. The Hebrew story of the exodus describes God working in partnership with Moses to lead the Hebrew slaves on a journey full of hardship and struggle to a promised land. Both the resurrection and the exodus are about God entering into experiences of suffering and being present in a complex process of give-and-take that brings new life.

These and other religious stories and symbols offer theological ways of understanding the process of empathy in pastoral care. God can be experienced as present within the caregiving relationship, in much the same way that God was believed to be present in the stories describing exodus and resurrection. This kind of presence helps to establish a relationship of trust. In the opening illustration, Sam Lee is able to create a safe place for Mrs. Wood to express her confusion, anger, and sadness because he is empathetic to her concerns. He does not become overinvolved with or disengaged from Mrs. Wood. The trust that results from her sense of safety allows for some risks to be taken and mistakes made. Sam Lee's offer to say a prayer at the end of his meeting with Mrs. Wood could be experienced by her as insensitive. At this point in the conversation, Mrs. Wood feels safe enough to assert her own needs: "I'm sorry, Rev. Lee. I know I should have you say a prayer. I just don't feel comfortable with that right now." Sam Lee is able to affirm her for this: "You are an honest woman. That's good. I will see you again, I hope." His empathy is a key ingredient in establishing trust in this pastoral care relationship.

Power Dynamics

A second key ingredient in pastoral care relationships is power, which functions in tandem with relational dynamics. In describing the extremes of becoming disengaged or fused in caregiving relationships, we must talk about power dynamics and how differences in power can lead to the abuse of power. For example, if Sam Lee feels overpowered by Mrs. Wood's anger and confusion, he may become both disengaged and helpless, falling silent and not knowing how to respond. If he does this, he may well neglect her. Or, if he feels defensive and angry, he may assert his own agenda, lecturing on how she needs to claim her Korean ethnicity and religion. Pastoral caregivers need to learn how to recognize and monitor the power dynamics in caregiving relationships.

Power is always a feature of relationships, hence the term "power dynamics." I use the term "dynamic" to refer to processes going on within and between people, that is, patterns involving power that occur in relationships. Equal relationships can occur among those who are peers, such as friends, marital partners, peer colleagues, and siblings. In such relationships, people alternate between the two healthy poles of asserting themselves and recognizing the needs of the other.

When one person in a relationship is in the role of minister, rabbi, parent, or teacher, there is a difference in power. There are healthy ways for pastoral caregivers to use their power in caregiving relationships. In the pastoral care conversation between Sam Lee and Mrs. Wood, he let her take the lead in the conversation. He supported her sense of self-agency by, for example, affirming her response to his offer of prayer and leaving it up to her to decide if she would come back. He also affirmed her emotional responses, for example, her fears that she or her mother would be judged within a Korean congregation.

Sam Lee would have misused his power if he had become directive with Mrs. Wood. For instance, he might have insisted upon saying a prayer because that is how he always ends his meetings. He might have acted upon feelings of being attracted to Mrs. Wood by trying to give her a hug when she left. Alternatively, he could have felt overwhelmed by her anger and confusion, and remained silent or responded in highly tentative ways. Or he might have wanted to become friends with her, by telling her stories about how he also felt judged by the older Korean women in his congregation. If Sam Lee monitors his reactions to Mrs. Wood, he can recognize these potential responses and stop himself from acting impulsively on feelings of helplessness or desires to take charge.

Power Dynamics and Maps of Creation

Two contrasting theological understandings, or maps, of creation involve differing conceptions of how power functions in relationships. The first map of creation depicts a fixed hierarchical ordering of creation, which I describe metaphorically as the chain of being. The second map of creation describes an interconnected web of relationships in which differences in power are not fixed. Rather, they are part of the roles that people assume, changing over time.

Some religious traditions describe creation as a hierarchical order created by a transcendent being. Differences in power are understood as ontological or natural, that is, having to do with how God created the world. Historically, many religious traditions, for example, Jewish, Christian, and Confucian traditions, are based upon this understanding of creation.

Biblical pastoral counseling is a current model of pastoral care that uses Christian sources of authority, like the Hebrew and New Testament Scriptures, to support a hierarchical understanding of creation. In this model, pastoral care is understood as a form of guidance that requires careseekers to submit themselves to the authority of those above them in the chain of being. In an illustration of such pastoral care, Jay Adams (1986) depicts a minister chastising a woman for coming to him for help before she sought help from her husband.

Natural or ontological hierarchies can be experienced as benevolent. In order to assess benevolence, caregivers need to imagine what it is like to be on the margins. Some liberation theologians most value the perspectives of those at the bottom, writing their theology from "the underside" (Thistlethwaite and Engel 1990). From this perspective, they are more likely to see an oppressive hierarchy, not a benevolent one. The collective sinfulness of human beings is such that ontological power differentials (i.e., husbands over wives, mothers-in-law over daughters-in-law) can too easily lead to abuse of power, which dehumanizes people. Those lower in the hierarchy are treated as less than human.

One way to use authority benevolently within an ontological hierarchy is to practice an overarching norm in which all people are seen as equally submissive to God's authority. For example, Christians seeking the benevolent use of ontological authority determined by gender may use Pauline texts about wives submitting to their husbands. They argue for husbands and wives being equally submissive to God's authority, and that such submission will make wives' submission to their husbands benevolent. In this way, they argue, submission, an essential aspect of an ontological hierarchy, becomes Spirit-led and graceful.

If sources and norms concerning sacred texts are used to establish an ontological ordering such that women are always submissive to men, then women may not assume equal leadership alongside men and may be seen instead as having complementary ministries. In some religious groups, rulings may have been made giving women positions of authority equal to men, but communities and governing bodies of faith may not yet be able to put these rulings into practice, because of their reluctance to accept these new roles of authority for women. The norm that limits women's authority in relation to men's overrides the norm that allows women to be ordained.

Many religious traditions have supported ontological hierarchies. At the same time, however, within many of these traditions, texts and/or practices exist that suggest alternate understandings of creation. For example, Ruth and Naomi, in the book of Ruth in the Hebrew Scriptures, form a partnership without the fixed power differences that traditionally existed between a mother-in-law and a daughter-in-law. The female lover in the Song of Songs is radically different from women of her time, entering into a mutual relationship with her lover in which she can express her sexual desires. Jesus is depicted in the Gospels as calling women to be his followers. The radical ways in which these stories challenged the chain of being was obscured by interpretations that maintained a "natural" fixed or static hierarchical order.

In the pastoral care conversation between Sam Lee and Mrs. Wood, Sam does not understand creation hierarchically by, for example, experiencing Mrs. Wood as disrespectful when she asks him not to pray. He does not inquire about her husband and his authority in their marriage. He does not treat Mrs. Wood in sexist ways by assuming that all women in crisis are confused and angry because they become fused in their relationships. He does not act in patronizing ways, by saying, for example, that her remark about sin and sex shows that she has not read current information about the church's understanding of sex. Instead, he respects her, and affirms the importance of her feelings and understanding of what is going on in her relationship with her mother. When she describes her horror at finding out that her mother was a prostitute, he affirms her feelings of being shocked and acknowledges her fears about her mother's being judged by those in the church. He commends her honesty.

The second map of creation, a web of being, stands in contrast to a hierarchical ontology or chain of being, emphasizes the mutual interconnectedness of creation, and uses the metaphor of web to describe creation.[2] In this map, creation can be pictured as more like a spider's web than a ladder, and the term "web of being" describes the complex interconnectedness among parts of creation. Within this map of creation, power differentials are not predetermined but are created when people enter into positions of responsibility over others that give them authority.[3] As Ramsay (1998, 114) notes, "Authority emerges from a web of relationships and is entrusted to another for the well-being of the whole."

When we understand God as all-powerful, the map of creation we use is a chain of being. In a chain of being, when innocent people suffer, people of religious faith ask why God allows such suffering. Understanding God's power in terms of a web of being is more challenging, since for many people God's omnipotence has been a cornerstone of their beliefs. Many theologians addressing this issue describe God, or a transcendent being, working in partnership with people and creation. Pastoral theologians, drawing upon process theology, describe God's power in terms of a web of being in which God's power is experienced in the partnership and within the web and can be described as power with, and not over, others (Cooper-White 1995, 2003; Graham 1992).

When pastoral caregivers monitor the power dynamics and relational boundaries during pastoral care conversations, they will become more aware of how their life experiences may induce anxiety, causing them to merge their experiences with the careseeker's and/or emotionally disengage. The ability to reflect upon one's own story is an essential moment of pastoral care and is discussed in the next chapter.

---

2. See Miller-McLemore (1996) for a description of how this metaphor represents contemporary pastoral theology among liberal pastoral theologians, both Protestant and Roman Catholic.

3. "Relational theorists have begun to reframe this difference in roles [of caregiver-careseeker] from one of hierarchy to one of *asymmetry*. While the participants share a mutuality of subjective experience, there is nevertheless an asymmetry in their respective roles and responsibilities" (Cooper-White 2003, 59).

2

The Caregiver's Life Experience as a Source of Authority

Now I describe the second step, or move, in this method of pastoral care. Caregivers who listen carefully and empathically to the stories told by persons seeking care inevitably find themselves hearing their own stories, as we see illustrated by Sam Lee's experience when he listens to Mrs. Wood's stories.

Sam Lee shares his experiences with a colleague, Jay Kim. Both men are in their mid- to late forties and emigrated to the United States in order to study for the ministry. They meet regularly with a group of pastoral caregivers for peer supervision. Sam joined this group after he had been in therapy. This group became quite meaningful to Sam, and he used it to monitor his responses to careseekers.

In preparation for this meeting, Sam Lee wrote a verbatim of his conversation with Mrs. Wood. A verbatim is a tool developed in clinical pastoral education in which caregivers re-create a pastoral care conversation from notes they have taken immediately afterwards and then reflect psychologically and theologically (a fuller description will be provided at the conclusion of this chapter). After Sam shares his experience with Mrs. Wood, he and Jay Kim discuss this session. As you review this, look for the ways Sam's story becomes a resource as he reflects upon his reactions to Mrs. Wood.

Jay Kim (1): I must say that I felt sad when I read about Mrs.

Wood's mother. I was also aware of how easy it is to judge her as a young woman who worked in a bar and went out with American soldiers. Instead of judging, however, I thought about the social conditions in Korea and how poverty sometimes made prostitution the only way to support one's family during the Korean War. Of course, the presence of American soldiers created the market for women who worked in the so-called entertainment industry.

Sam Lee (1): You understand the situation well.

Jay Kim (2): Yes. I've tried to educate myself. I used to understand sin as personal wrongdoing. Now I'm trying to see the social circumstances that are part of human sinfulness.

Sam Lee (2): I also had to struggle with an immediate response of judging Mrs. Wood's mother. It is strange how much, as you say, I sometimes react the way my parents might.

Jay Kim (3): Your judgment doesn't come through in the conversation.

Sam Lee (3): I'm glad to hear you say that. I was concerned about it.

Jay Kim (4): I found it remarkable how well you did listen to her.

Sam Lee (4): Well, it would have been much harder if her mother had come to me, instead of Mrs. Wood.

Jay Kim (5): How so?

Sam Lee (5): Well, Mrs. Wood reminds me of my daughters, even though she's about ten years older than they are. She has no accent. She seems wholly American. I could relate to her the way I now try to relate to my daughters.

Jay Kim (6): So this is how you talk with your daughters?

Sam Lee (6): It's how I try to talk with them. It isn't easy. I went through some terrible struggles with them a few years ago.

Jay Kim (7): Yes, I remember how I struggled with my parents. They wanted me to live out their wishes, like going to Harvard instead of University of Massachusetts.

Sam Lee (7): With my daughters, they wanted to make their own choices, just as you did. My wife and I were protective of them, telling them when to be home, and whom to date. We wanted them to date the men in the church. They rebelled, and said we were old-fashioned, and that we didn't understand them. My daughters teamed up one time and sat down with me and talked about their struggles with me. I was so upset that I had to talk with a counselor. He helped me really hear how much my daughters had suffered and how hard it was for them to talk to me.

Jay Kim (8): That sounds difficult.

Sam Lee (8): It was. I had to go back to my own teenage years and remember what it was like with my father. He was the minister of a large congregation in Korea, and he was a stern minister to me, not really a father. I had to obey him. My brother didn't, and it was terrible in the church. My brother has had so many problems. He drinks a lot. I wonder if he hits his wife. This bothers me.

Jay Kim (9): I'm sorry to hear about your brother. So you had to be the good son.

Sam Lee (9): Yes. That's why I became a minister initially. My father wanted me to go to the seminary of one of his mentors. I started there and then realized it was really too conservative for me. So I switched to a more theologically liberal college. He was really disappointed.

Jay Kim (10): I understand how all of these memories of him must have come back when your daughters talked to you about their troubles as teenagers.

Sam Lee (10): Yes. It all seems so vivid as we talk about it.

Jay Kim (11): Yes. (Silence.) So that's the story behind this conversation with Mrs. Wood.

Sam Lee (11): You know, I was able to listen to her much better than I can listen to my own daughters. It's still hard. But Mrs. Wood wasn't angry with me, and I wasn't related to her. Somehow, I could be much more understanding, maybe too understanding. I felt so warmly towards her.

Jay Kim (12): That's something we can talk about. Let's look through the conversation again, and look at your efforts to connect with her.

In his conversation with Jay Kim, Sam is able to be self-disclosive. Notice how he gives Jay enough information about his story so that Jay can see how Sam's story is connected to this pastoral care conversation. Sam has worked through these aspects of his story so that he doesn't need Jay to be his counselor. If Sam hadn't done this work, then it would be much harder for him to recognize how his personal story connected with his conversation with Mrs. Wood.

The work he has done in personal therapy on conflicts with his daughters and memories of his father allows him to use one healthy identity he has, that of a good father. He learned that it is important to reflect with someone about his work as a pastoral caregiver. In his conversation with Jay Kim, he has the self-knowledge as well as the psychological and theological knowledge to look further at the liabilities of casting Mrs. Wood in the role of daughter and himself in the role of an older male relative.

Sam Lee's Transformative Experience

When Sam's daughters confronted him about his relationship with them, he went into a tailspin. He felt they were disrespectful, treating him as an equal rather than a father. He imagined that his own father would have had a heart attack if Sam had talked to him as an equal. He was angry that they couldn't understand that he and his wife were protecting them, and angry that they weren't respecting their parents' wishes.

His reaction to their confrontation caused stress, and he realized in retrospect that he responded by working harder at the church, as if to prove that he was a good father to the church family, even if he wasn't to his daughters. He began to have difficulty sleeping and often felt exhausted. His annual physical exam came around, and he complained to his physician, Dr. David Oh, about his sleeping problems. David Oh wisely asked whether anything was troubling Sam. At first Sam talked about the work at church. David Oh did not simply see workaholism as a necessary aspect of professional life. So he asked about what was going on at home. Much to Sam's surprise, he found himself describing his daughters' confrontation. He expected the doctor to sympathize, even though David Oh was quite a bit younger than he was, and felt somewhat affronted when David Oh suggested that he might talk to a counselor about the situation. Sam explained that he didn't need that kind of help; anyway, a psychologist wouldn't understand the cultural and religious issues. David Oh acknowledged that he did not know of any Korean American pastoral counselors, but urged him to see a pastoral counselor and recommended an older Anglo-American male counselor named Dr. Andrew Caulder. He concluded by saying that he would rather not prescribe sleeping pills yet, and asked Sam to check back with him and let him know if the counseling was helpful.

Though it was hard, Sam did call Andrew Caulder. At first, he didn't want to talk about his family situation, and Andrew seemed to understand this. He let Sam go at his own pace. They talked about his sleeping problems and how this affected his work. Sam began to see that he was working too hard, and he made the connections between this and how he was avoiding his stressful family life. Over time, Sam acknowledged both his conflicts with his daughters and his memories of his father.

Andrew and Sam brought Sam's devotional life into their counseling. Sam began to focus his prayers and biblical studies on his experiences with his daughters and his father. Andrew suggested that Sam pray to a God who is a loving, gentle father. While Sam could accept this image intellectually, he realized he scorned a father like that. It was hard for him to combine gentleness and authority. As he concentrated his spiritual activities on experiencing God as father in new ways, these new images of God became more real, perhaps in part because he experienced Andrew as using his authority in gentle and caring ways.

A turning point came when Andrew suggested that he bring his wife and daughters in for some sessions. At first Sam refused, too ashamed of talking openly with them. With Andrew's help, he was gradually able to access a range of feelings—not just fear and anger—when he was with his daughters. These meetings helped Sam learn how to listen and communicate with his family. When his therapy was nearing an end, Andrew suggested that Sam join a peer supervision group.

Sam's Story as a Resource in His Care of Mrs. Wood

Knowing more about Sam's story, we can return to considering the ways in which his story has the potential to limit or enhance his pastoral care of Mrs. Wood. I will draw upon the concepts of relational boundaries and power dynamics introduced in chapter 1 to reflect upon the similarities and differences between Sam's and Mrs. Wood's stories, and the likelihood of Sam being empathic, disengaged from, or merged with Mrs. Wood. I will consider their common experience of being Korean Americans, the generational difference between Sam as an immigrant and Mrs. Wood as the daughter of an immigrant, their gender difference, and the possibility of differences or similarities in their theological orientations.

Common themes in both Sam's and Mrs. Wood's narratives are the losses and gains of emigration from Korea to the United States. They each have experienced the cross-cultural gains of being part of two cultures. Sam may be more aware of these gains than Mrs. Wood because he works within the Korean context of the congregation. Mrs. Wood may be less able to value her Korean heritage because of the circumstances of her parents' marriage, in which it is likely that this heritage has been devalued.

Both have experienced the losses of being part of extended families that stretch across the Pacific Ocean. Mrs. Wood's relationships with her Korean extended family may well be strained by her mother's interracial marriage and her family's judgment of her. Her Korean extended family may be ashamed of her mother's marriage. Sam also experiences the loss of his extended family. He experiences the strains of being a son who is less able to fulfill his filial duties of caring for his Korean parents because he is in the United States. Each may, in different ways, experience *han*, a Korean term describing the complex suffering of those who are marginalized (Park 1993, 1996). One difference between their immigration stories is that Sam chose to come to the United States, a decision based on the opportunity of further education. Mrs. Wood's mother may not have felt as though she had much choice, given the marginalized social status she would have had if she had remained in Korea.

Another complex issue related to their immigration stories is their experience of racism. They both have been at the receiving end of racial prejudice. Unlike Mrs. Wood, Sam may have experienced prejudice at moments because English is not his native language. This discussion of Sam's and Mrs. Wood's stories of immigration highlights the ways in which subtle differences exist alongside overarching commonalities. How might these commonalities and subtle difference affect Sam's reactions to Mrs. Wood?

One benefit of Sam's therapy and his ongoing reflections in his peer supervision group is that he can now access deep feelings of sadness at the heart of his experience of immigration. In reflecting upon his relationship with his father, he realized that he is able to mourn the losses of immigration in ways his father never could and that he carries his father's as well as his own grief. His awareness of this grief is a resource as he listens to Mrs. Wood and is attuned to the losses of immigration that have been part of her and her mother's stories. Hearing about the marriage of Mrs. Wood's parents, Sam comments (*Rev. Lee [4]*) that it sounds so sad, and soon after Mrs. Wood cries in sorrow as she tells the story of how her parents met. Later, when he meets with Jay Kim to share the verbatim, Jay's first remark (*Jay Kim [1]*) is that he felt sad when he read about Mrs. Wood's mother. Both men can identify with the sadness of Mrs. Wood's story because they are aware of the various losses they and their families experienced as a result of immigration.

This awareness of sadness goes hand in hand with Sam Lee's profound moments of joy that sometimes overtake him when he is in the midst of ministry with Korean members of the congregation or when he delights in some aspect of his life in America. In his brief encounter with Mrs. Wood he notices her opening remark (*Mrs. Wood [1]*), that she thought "it would be strangely comforting to worship in a Korean congregation." He realizes that such worship is an encounter with her Korean heritage that helps her access her feelings of sadness, and that she seems not to experience joy and delight in her heritage. While he could easily become merged with her, wanting her to have his experiences of taking delight in his heritage, and directive in urging her to return to a Korean church, he simply expresses his hope that he will see her again (*Rev. Lee [14]*).

In therapy Sam was able to transform his relationship with his father, a relationship shaped by theological differences and the stresses of immigration. He gained a new respect for his father, especially when he realized that his father struggled the way Sam did as a father with his daughters. Without this newly gained respect he could, in listening to Mrs. Wood, easily become disengaged from and judgmental of her mother. Instead he empathized with her mother, and suggested that she protected her daughter from the harsh realities of her mother's history (*Rev. Lee [9]*). He finds support for his empathic understanding when Jay Kim shares his perceptions of what it must have been like for Mrs. Wood (*Jay Kim [1]*).

The gender differences in this pastoral care relationship could easily result in Sam Lee's being emotionally disengaged from Mrs. Wood by projecting upon her his ideal of Korean womanhood. In his struggles with his daughters he became aware of how painful it was for them to become persons in their own right in relation to parents who believed in traditional Korean family values. He is sensitive to the even more complex struggles of Mrs. Wood, growing up in a cross-racial marriage in which her mother's culture was devalued. Her rejection of his offer of prayer, which could replicate his daughters' rejection of his authority, is met with his affirmation of her honesty (*Rev. Lee [14]*). Aware of these gender and generational differences, he reflects with Jay Kim on his relationship with Mrs. Wood and his daughters.

One final difference that is not explicit in the pastoral care conversation concerns theological orientation. His initial reference to God—(*Rev. Lee [4]*) "Their marriage was so sad. Not what God wants for us"—was met with silence, giving Sam no indication of Mrs. Wood's response to this use of theological language. Shortly afterwards, Mrs. Wood alludes to possible differences when she says (*Mrs. Wood [8]*), "Well, you are a minister. And sin is all about sex. I'm sorry. I'm more American than Korean." In his reply Sam sidesteps an explicit discussion of their possible differences, commenting on what it must have been like for her mother. In the process he demonstrates that he is not judging her mother in the ways that Mrs. Wood fears. Later, when Mrs. Wood confesses (*Mrs. Wood [11]*) that she was afraid to come to him because he's a Korean minister, the issue of potential theological differences is again on the table. Sam replies with an acknowledgment of her fear and self-disclosure about his children and how they have taught him to be a better listener (*Rev. Lee [11]*). These exchanges merit further reflection in his conversation with Jay Kim.

In not directly addressing the issue of their potential theological differences Sam may have intuitively guessed that there was not a sufficient level of trust to venture into the arena of theological convictions about sin and sex. His investment in maintaining a connection, fueled perhaps by similar investments with his daughters, may have made him anxious about conflict. His awareness of his relationship with his daughters is evident in his self disclosure that they have taught him to be a good listener. When, near the end, he offers to pray with her (*Rev. Lee [13]*) and she describes her discomfort, it seems that his earlier hunch—that potential theological differences were too risky to address—is confirmed. Sam could easily have felt compelled to initiate a discussion about his theology in an effort to convince her of their similarities. The urgency of such a discussion would likely be fueled by his anxieties about being connected with his daughters. He is able to set this agenda aside and follow Mrs. Wood's lead. In reflecting with Jay Kim about whether and how to engage in theological reflection with

Mrs. Wood, Sam will be better prepared to monitor this issue if Mrs. Wood returns for another conversation.

Sam's pastoral care conversation with Mrs. Wood becomes the occasion for exploring his reactions as he prepares a verbatim and later discusses it with Jay Kim. The potential for him to become a better pastoral caregiver is realized in these opportunities for self-reflection. While he initially provided care to Mrs. Wood, he in turn received care in his consultation with Jay Kim and in the process became more deeply connected with himself, those for whom he cared, and God.

In chapter 3, I examine how the verbal responses of caregivers, their tone of voice, their eye contact, their facial expressions, and their body language can shape the caregiving relationship. This discussion of the "nuts and bolts" of listening may seem like a detour, a pause in the description of the steps taken in pastoral care. Rather than a pause, however, this discussion is an elaboration of how to listen in ways that communicate the deepest beliefs of caregivers. Without such discussion, caregivers will not be able to embody their beliefs and represent the kind of transformative presence that enables healing and justice in their own lives and in the lives of others. Without such embodiment and representation, healing and justice will be short-circuited when the caregiver's operational beliefs evident in verbal responses and body language reflect the tragic limitations experienced by the caregiver in his or her formative years.

EXERCISE 1: WRITING A VERBATIM

A verbatim is a script of a pastoral care conversation. While any conversation in which you offer help could be construed as a pastoral care conversation, strictly speaking, such conversations occur when you are acting as a representative of your religious tradition—perhaps as a chaplain or minister in training—and there is an explicit or implicit agreement that you will provide pastoral care to someone who has sought your help.

This exercise will guide you through the process of writing a verbatim. As soon as possible after the conversation is over, make notes detailing the flow of the conversation, especially the points when transitions occur that shift the focus or go more deeply into a topic. In preparing the script of the conversation, number each response for easy reference, labeling the pastor's first statement as (1) and the careseeker's first statemei   ve a three-inch margin on the right-hand side for comments.

After you   tten the verbatim, introduce it with two sets of comments.

— Under the first heading (Known facts) summarize what you knew about the careseeker before beginning the conversation. Describe the circumstances in which the conversation took place.

— Under the next heading (Observations) describe what you notice about the physical location, the careseeker's physical appearance, body language, and emotional reactions, and your body language and emotional reactions during the conversation.

EXERCISE 2: SELF-REFLECTION

Having prepared and introduced the script, you will now reflect upon your pastoral care conversation in a series of exercises that are described at the end of each of the next seven chapters.

The first reflection concerns your story. Using the following guidelines, explore in writing whether aspects of your own story are resources or roadblocks to you in this pastoral care conversation.

— Describe any experiences you have had that are similar to the careseeker's circumstances or crisis.

— Reflect on the extent to which the similarities or differences between your story and the careseeker's may be a resource, in terms of helping you empathize.

— How might each similarity or difference make it likely that you will (1) become emotionally merged with or disengaged from the careseeker; (2) become helpless because of feeling overpowered; and/or (3) become directive because you need to be in control? Reference specific responses in the verbatim that illustrate the dynamics you describe.

3

Listening

Caregivers who have done the psychological and spiritual work of transforming their earlier restrictive images of God and self, and become comfortable with different ways to use their bodies and voices, can work creatively with the increasingly complex and varied relationships they form with careseekers. They will be able to fine-tune the way they communicate, especially with people from different cultures. A caregiver may know or intuit, for example, that shaking a careseeker's hand at the end of a meeting may communicate a warm way of saying good-bye to some people, a stiff, formal farewell to others, and an intrusion with still others. Caregivers can expand the ways in which they use their bodies and their verbal responses to a range that feels authentic. They can take their cues from what they know psychologically and culturally about those seeking care, and also what they experience in terms of the careseeker's style of communication.

Some of you may be suspicious of this emphasis on communication skills. You may know sales and marketing professionals, for instance, who have invested in improving communication skills in order to sell their products and increase their individual productivity. Their slick presentations often seem inauthentic. The important difference is that pastoral caregivers can distinguish cultural from theological reasons for improving communication skills. Caregivers want the theology they communicate through their facial expressions and body to be congruent with their beliefs. Given that a degree of the theology they communicate through their bodies may be unconscious, formed in childhood and intense crises, caregivers may need to do some deep self-reflections. Working on communication skills can be an intense spiritual experience for a caregiver who finds it hard to be with people in a way that expresses her or his deliberative beliefs.

In reflecting upon congruency between a caregiver's body language and his or her beliefs, I highlight the important role of authenticity. Authenticity requires at a basic level that caregivers understand what they may be communicating in how they listen and in their tone of voice and body language. Ramsay (1998, chapter 4), writing on the responsibilities associated with the pastoral caregiving role, observes that authenticity "in the practice of ministry reflects an interactive and evolving relational and theological competence" (Ramsay 2000, 278). This relational and theological competence evolves over time "as we participate in increasingly complex, embodied, and varied relational networks" (Ramsay 2000, 278). It has two elements: (1) how a caregiver understands his or her theology, and (2) how this theology is reflected in the caregiver's communication skills.

The following story illustrates how caregivers can work in a small learning group on issues having to do with the authenticity of their communication. Ralph, a young priest-in-training studying at a Roman Catholic seminary, practiced pastoral care by doing a role play of the sacrament of reconciliation, set in a small room with chairs at an angle to each other. As Joe, role-playing the parishioner, begins his confession, Ralph slouches in his chair and looks down. When asked by his teacher to try sitting up straight, leaning forward and maintaining eye contact with Joe, Ralph feels so anxious that he reverts to his habitual posture. He realizes that he is uncomfortable with being a priest who hears confessions in this face-to-face manner. His posture of slouching forward and looking down is a way of seeking privacy for himself and the careseeker. In reflecting on this role-play in a small group, he realizes that his body language reflects the sense of shame he experienced as a child during the sacrament of confession. His body language reflects this childhood experience and is at odds with his adult experience of a sense of grace that comes with confession. He feels sad that a sacrament meant to mediate God's grace exacerbated his feelings of shame as a child. His teacher suggests that he do the role-play again, and visualize bringing himself as a small boy into the room, imagining this boy sitting beside Ralph. This exercise helps Ralph separate from his childhood experience of confession so that he does not become merged with it or project it on the careseeker. He can access his adult beliefs and experiences concerning the grace of the sacrament, and his body language changes.

Responsive Communication

This illustration highlights the depth of reflection that can be part of working on communication skills. The first step in doing such work is to observe the habitual verbal responses one makes during pastoral care conversations, and see if these responses can be expanded. There are four kinds of responses that are part of communicating,[1] each of which I consider in the sections that follow:

—Paraphrasing what careseekers say in order to clarify meanings
—Asking clarifying questions
—Making interpretations about the careseeker's emotional state
—Knowing when and how to use appropriate self-disclosure

Paraphrasing for Clarification

Paraphrasing involves restating in your own words what you hear someone communicating. This strategy is especially useful in three situations. The first is when one is working with someone from a different culture. Caregivers can use this strategy to clarify the content of what is being communicated. The second is when the careseeker's pace of speech (too slow, too fast) and level of content (too many or too few details) makes it hard to get a big picture of what is going on. A third situation in which paraphrase is helpful is when caregivers are having difficulty paying attention to the content of what is being said. In our anxiety to understand quickly, we may be busy constructing hypotheses without listening to details. Paraphrasing forces us to pay attention.

In order to paraphrase, a caregiver must pay careful attention to details, sorting out key words and points made by the careseeker. Take, for example, the case of Anna, who has visited a worship service and asks to see Rev. Mugabe after church. She begins by telling him that she's been living in the area for two years, and has started visiting

---

1. Savage's (1996) *Listening and Caring Skills* and Egan's (1994) *The Skilled Helper* are helpful in gaining an overview of issues concerning communication.

neighborhood churches on Sunday mornings. She describes something about her church background, which is Protestant, and her lack of strong denominational affiliation. She notes that Joseph, her three-month-old son, is at home with her husband, Ray, and they are looking forward to a family visit at Thanksgiving from her out-of-town parents. Her parents have been asking when Joseph will be baptized. Anna is not sure where to have the baptism. At this point in the conversation, Rev. Mugabe may make a paraphrasing statement: "It sounds like you and your husband want to respond to your parents' desires to have their grandchild baptized." This simple paraphrase might help to focus the conversation on what the parents of this child want.

Asking Clarifying Questions

A clarifying question could be asked next. Rev. Mugabe could ask, "Setting aside your parents' wishes for the moment, do you and Ray want Joseph to be baptized?" Depending on how they have responded, he might follow up with, "How do you see this congregation's role in your family's life after the baptism?" Their response will clarify whether they understand baptism as a family ritual for celebrating their child's birth and/or as a ritual that welcomes their child into the life of this particular community of faith.

In their anxiety to be helpful, novice pastoral caregivers often ask more clarifying questions than are needed, and in the process neglect to communicate empathy through the use of paraphrasing responses or interpretations of the careseeker's emotional states. For example, it is not necessary for Rev. Mugabe to ask where this woman's parents live, or whether this is their first grandchild. While clarifying questions are needed later in the assessment phase of caregiving, caregivers must reflect upon the reasons they are asking questions and whose needs are being addressed by the questions. Do their questions have to do with the caregiver's anxious need to be helpful and appear to be in charge, or the caregiver's need to clarify information helpful for an assessment?

The depth of information sought by the caregiver needs to be appropriate in the cultural setting in which care takes place. "Setting aside your parents' wishes for the moment, do you and Ray want Joseph to be baptized?" and "How do you see this congregation's role in your family's life after the baptism?" are questions that are most culturally appropriate with Anglo-Americans, who are used to direct questions. This culture is low context; therefore, there is more explicit verbal communication and nothing is assumed. Rather than allow the careseeker's story to unfold gradually and allow time to establish connections by way of inquiries about family or through silence, many Anglo-Americans want to "get down to business" by asking direct questions, especially in business and professional settings.

Direct questions might not, however, be suitable to use with people who want first to invest in establishing a relationship with each other before "getting down to business." People from collectivist cultures, such as Latin America, Native American tribes, Africa, Asia, and Arab countries, often see people as interdependent members of a group (i.e., extended family or tribe) where collective survival is more important than individual survival (Okum, Fried, and Okum 1999, 12). In such settings, a caregiver might begin by getting to know the careseeker as a member of a family and community. Gaining background about the collective group may be more important initially than asking about the individual. This would often be the case for pastoral caregivers working on a reservation with members of a North American tribe. The careseeker may respond in seemingly circuitous ways to direct questions, and as a result may be labeled in negative ways by people from individualistic cultures. Anglo-American pastoral caregivers need to pay special attention to the effects of their communication styles on people from other cultures. Their lack of cultural sensitivity to differences in communication styles may be part of an Anglo-American pastoral caregivers' enactment of her or his white privilege, accrued from being part of a dominant culture (Ramsay 2002). They may fail to establish trust by being culturally sensitive to differences in communication styles and act in ways that are culturally insensitive and even racist.

Interpreting the Careseeker's Emotional State

A third listening strategy, making interpretations about the careseeker's emotional state, can help in assessing the depth and kind of suffering experienced by those seeking care and communicate the caregiver's compassion and empathy. While people universally experience basic emotions like anger, fear, sadness, pleasure, disgust, and surprise, and also use similar facial expressions (Ekman 1993; Poortinga, Shoots, and Van de Koppel 1993), cultural differences determine whether these feelings are kept private or openly displayed by facial expressions. In highly formal cultures, like many Asian cultures, keeping feelings private is important. Other cultures—such as the cultures of Italy and

Spain—value intense expression of particular feelings. Gender is a strong cultural factor when it comes to identifying what feelings are valuable and appropriate for men to express (like anger among Anglo-Americans) and what feelings are valuable and appropriate for women to express (such as fear).

The challenge of learning how to become culturally sensitive is that one may initially formulate what seem to be cultural stereotypes in becoming familiar with those from a different culture. Writing about introductory texts on multicultural counseling, Lartey comments,

> Some well-meaning attempts to inform counselors and other carers about "ethnic minority clients" adopted in many forms of "multi-cultural training" fall into this trap by perpetuating the myths, for example, about the angry underachieving Caribbean male; the Asian young woman's oppressive cultural role; the African student's problem with communication; the problems of the Asian extended family or the single-parent Caribbean family. As such, far from enabling attention to the particular client in question, these forms fuel stereotyping of the most heinous kind.
>
> (Lartey 2003, 32–33)

Lartey uses Kluckhohn and Murray's (1948) assertion that "Every person is in certain respects (1) like all others, (2) like some others, and (3) like no other" (Lartey 2003, 43) to argue that each careseeker will both reflect aspects of his or her culture and also be unique. He recommends an "intercultural" approach in which "the complex interrelatedness and interconnectedness of the three spheres interacting in living, growing and changing human persons is what is expected, treated as the norm and attended to" (Lartey 2003, 35). Pastoral caregivers providing care to persons from cultures unfamiliar to them may initially rely on broad descriptions of culture as they become sensitized to the subtle ways in which the careseeker is both like and unlike others in her or his culture. They must be cautious about acting in culturally insensitive ways as they are learning how to offer intercultural care.

Pastoral caregivers working in culturally homogeneous communities of faith may not experience a need for providing intercultural pastoral care. This need is greatest among pastoral caregivers in public institutions like hospitals, nursing homes, and hospice organizations, in which there is a higher likelihood of encountering people from different cultures. Even in homogenous settings, however, the need for intercultural pastoral care arises when members of the congregation struggle to understand those who are different. This need has been apparent in cross-cultural dialogues between Christians and Muslims in the aftermath of terrorist attacks.

The most likely scenario in which pastoral caregivers will engage in intercultural care is when communities of faith have significant numbers of members from minority cultures, or engage in outreach to persons from such cultures. In such settings, caregivers have the opportunity to encounter those from a different culture in more profound ways. Such encounters enhance the caregiver's ability to live on the boundary, able to appreciate the richness and otherness of their own and another's culture (Augsburger 1986).

Appropriate Self-Disclosure

A final verbal strategy is appropriate self-disclosure. Within a community of faith, caregivers may have various public roles, such as the leader of worship, the preacher, the teacher, as well as the caregiver. There are also occasions where caregivers socialize with careseekers. They may know each other's families or they may work together on committees, and rely upon each other for specific committee responsibilities. In such contexts, three characteristics of care are important when it comes to appropriate self-disclosure. Caregivers need to monitor which role they are in and know when they are being called to assume a caregiver role. The caregiver needs to ensure that it is the careseeker's needs that are being met in social settings when the caregiver is self-disclosive. Given the power differential between caregiver and careseeker, the needs of the latter come first. If the caregiver's needs eclipse the potential careseeker's, then the caregiver looks outside of the faith community in order to meet his or her needs. For example, a caregiver can let a careseeker struggling with alcoholism know that he, too, has been through a recovery program. However, if he goes on to describe all of the details of his recovery, then the attention may shift away from the careseeker. The careseeker may feel cast in the role of empathic listener.

Body Language and Use of Space

Caregivers can increase their effectiveness not only by reflecting upon their use of paraphrase, questions, interpretations, and self-disclosure.

They can also attend to habitual ways of using their tone of voice, facial expressions, and bodies when assuming a caregiving role, as well as their management of time and space. Do they often work with a time frame of twenty-five or fifty minutes when meeting with people seeking care? Do they meet people in their homes, or is pastoral care done during scheduled appointments at the church? How are the chairs arranged in the office? Do they directly face each other, or are they set at an angle? Is the door open or closed? Is there anyone else in the building? These are the types of questions that caregivers can explore in reflecting upon how they manage time and space. By being aware of their habits, care-givers can experiment with the ways they use their body, their space, and their time so that they have choices that authentically reflect their beliefs about healing and justice-seeking relationships. Having such choices can be of great benefit in responding to people from various types of families and cultures and with differing personality styles. The following two scenarios illustrate strategies for reflecting upon one's use of space and body language.

Example 1

Ruben, a student in rabbinic studies, videotaped himself while he was doing a role-play of a caregiving conversation with Tom. He was surprised at how distant his voice sounded and how measured his pace of words. Without much thought, he had arranged the role-play so that his chair was against the same wall as Tom's and both were turned slightly toward each other. When he sat facing forward, he was positioned to look out of the window, and he had to turn his body and head to have eye contact with Tom. This body language and use of space satisfied Tom, but when another student, Sarah, was cast in the role of careseeker, she felt frustrated because she had to twist in her chair and lean forward to engage Ruben more directly. It reminded her of how hard it was to get her father's attention when she was a little girl.

Ruben found this feedback revelatory. He asked himself what his body language and use of space said about how God was present for him and the careseeker. He did more role-plays in which the chairs were turned toward each other and he sat forward, maintained more eye contact, and varied his tone of voice and pace to express more warmth. He was surprised at how anxiety-provoking this was, even in the role-play. In talking with some of his friends in rabbinic studies, he realized this anxiety was similar to childhood feelings about needing to fend off his mother in order to attain some privacy. Reflecting theologically, he decided to reflect further on what this anxiety might be saying about his relationships with his mother, God, and careseekers. In a field education placement he developed specific goals for his pastoral care visits, goals that had to do with communicating his beliefs through his body language. He talked with his supervisor about how he could reach these goals, and they used verbatim accounts of some of his visits to help his learning process.

Example 2

When Zena, an African American student in a class on pastoral care, watched a video role-play of herself as caregiver, she realized how soft-spoken she was, no matter what the content of the conversation, and that she gave many verbal affirmations to Eun-Soo, a Korean American male student playing the role of careseeker. Zena continually nodded her head, making sounds to indicate that she was listening. Eun-Soo experienced this as distracting and wondered why she needed to agree so vehemently with everything he said. In theologically reflecting upon his feedback, she wondered if she was trying to communicate God's continual presence that creates a holding space for caregiver and careseeker. She commented that she was trying to do all the relational holding of the careseeker with her voice, facial expression, and body language. She was not trusting that God and Eun-Soo were also participating in creating a holding environment. In a group discussion with other African American women in her class, she realized that her body language expressed formative beliefs about being self-reliant and not trusting anyone but herself to provide care. She began spiritual practices focused on images of a web of being of which her caring was a part. She used these images so that, in caregiving role-plays, she varied her tone of voice, especially with careseekers who might need more of a sense of separation than connection.

Physical Contact

Physical contact—specifically handshakes and hugs—also plays a significant role in communication. Such physical contact in public places, while needing to be monitored, is much less likely to be misunderstood or used in ways that are or can be experienced as intrusive.

A hug initiated by a caregiver that takes place in a private space is much more likely to arouse anxiety and be interpreted by the careseeker as an expression of sexual intimacy. When careseeker or caregiver feels the urge to initiate a hug, it is important to identify the relational dynamics at both conscious and unconscious levels. When careseekers initiate a hug, caregivers need to make a split-second decision about how to respond, and then talk with the careseeker about what he or she was trying to communicate through physical contact. These incidents can be reflected upon further in conversations with colleagues, and such conversations are a way of being accountable for the use of physical contact in caregiving relationships.

Issues of physical contact can be particularly sensitive in a cross-cultural context, such as a hospital setting in which caregivers visit patients from many cultures and religious traditions. For example, in providing care to patients who are about to go into surgery, hospital chaplain Edward Rothschild visits a Muslim woman whose head is covered. He limits his eye contact with her, responding to her downcast look. Similarly, in visiting another presurgery patient, a Hindu man from India, Rothschild observes how Haroun greets him, by placing his hands together as if in prayer, raising his hands to his forehead and bowing. Edward can follow suit, responding in a similar manner. Respecting cultural norms about physical contact between a caregiver and careseeker is part of establishing an empathic relationship.

Privacy of Space

A final aspect of communication is creating space that is comfortable and safe for both careseekers and caregivers. Many ministers who meet with careseekers in their office have arrangements that afford privacy for the careseeker and make the caregiver visible, by leaving the office door ajar or having a window in the door, and seating careseekers with their backs to the door. Gender differences between careseeker and caregiver usually make this physical arrangement a more sensitive issue. Caregivers need to decide on a range of options with which they feel comfortable and discuss these options with colleagues and people in leadership positions in the organizations and communities of faith where they work. For example, a new priest may discuss with the vestry the congregation's tradition concerning clergy doing home visits. They may together decide that such visits are appropriate for elderly parishioners who are housebound or for family meetings. They may see whether the priest can arrange for other visits in his office, when other staff members are around. These discussions can clarify the expectations of caregivers and members of communities of faith, and also identify what aspects of the privacy of visits need to be altered, given a growing awareness of sexual misconduct.

As pastoral caregivers listen to the stories told by those seeking care and to the stories evoked within themselves, they use their verbal responses and bodies in ways that reflect their deepest beliefs about transcendent realities. Congruency between caregivers' actions and beliefs is essential. Without it, caregivers cannot be certain that the care they offer is, indeed, care that seeks healing and justice. If their care reflects false beliefs formed through unredeemed experiences of pain and suffering—for example, beliefs that suffering can ultimately separate them from any transcendent reality that brings healing and justice—then the care they offer may ultimately reflect this despair. While the work of reflecting deeply upon one's beliefs and how these beliefs may be reflected in caregiving relationships does not happen overnight, a long-term commitment to monitoring this core issue of pastoral care can lead to a deepening authenticity across diverse and complex caregiving relationships.

EXERCISE 3: REFLECTING ON LISTENING SKILLS

Review the verbatim prepared in exercise 1 in chapter 2, identifying your responses: paraphrasing; asking questions; making interpretations about the careseeker's emotional state; knowing when and how to use appropriate self-disclosure. Reflect upon which types of responses you favored. Did you favor any particular response because of your needs or the careseeker's needs? Did this type of response help you stay closely attuned with the careseeker? If not, what response would have worked better?

See if you can recall your bodily reactions throughout the pastoral care conversation. At any moments did you draw closer or lean back, slump down or sit up, cross your arms over your chest or let your arms relax, clench your jaw or tighten your shoulder muscles, or suddenly let tensed muscles relax? How do you understand these bodily reactions in terms of the process that was taking place in the pastoral care conversation?

Reflect upon the seating arrangements and the space in which this conversation took place. Did this seating arrangement and the space help you stay connected with the careseeker, while giving her or him and you enough space apart to feel comfortable? Is there anything you might change, if you could, that would have made this a better space for your conversation?

4

Establishing a Caregiving Relationship

Sally Brown, a student intern at Rocky Mountain United Methodist Church, is given the assignment of visiting elderly, housebound members. When she arrives at the apartment of Louise Haverly, she is uneasy about the state of disorder she finds. The living room is filled with piles of old newspapers and bags full of odds and ends. Louise invites her to sit at the kitchen table. Surveying the sticky floor, stacks of dirty dishes, and cartons of leftover food, Sally regrets accepting Louise's offer of tea and tries not to look too closely at the mug Louise hands her. Louise asks several times why she has come and inquires about the former minister, unaware that he left two years ago. When Sally asks whether Louise has family members who visit, Louise vaguely refers to a nephew but is unclear when they were last in contact. Sally notices several recent scars on Louise's hands and wonders if she burned herself while cooking. Sally is unsure how closely to question Louise about her ability to care for herself. She brings these concerns to the next session with her field education supervisor. They plan to visit Louise together and get more information about her medical care and when her last physical examination was. Sally's supervisor hopes to get permission from Louise to talk to her physician during their visit. They want to find out if it is safe for Louise to live by herself.

The next step of pastoral care has to do with establishing an initial contract for care that reflects professional and ecclesial codes of conduct

47

and ensures that careseekers will not be harmed. Sally's first concern is Louise's physical well-being. She needs to know the parameters of the care she can offer, including the limits of confidentiality and her expertise, which are aspects of an implicit contract of care. While contracts for care are not usually explicitly negotiated in pastoral relationships as they are in psychotherapeutic ones, caregivers must still attend to relevant issues concerning professional conduct and, when appropriate, discuss these issues with careseekers. Such discussions might take place, for example, when there are limits to confidentiality or when issues concerning the availability of the caregiver need to be clarified. For example, Sally's supervisor will explain to Louise that she is concerned about her well-being and wants permission to consult her physician.

The establishment of a pastoral care relationship in which careseekers will not be harmed is a basic aspect of care for which caregivers are accountable. Accountability involves being responsible for offering care that meets ecclesial, professional, and legal standards. More than simply a professional requirement and inevitable aspect of the increasing professionalization of ministry, accountability to codes of conduct can be understood theologically as part of living out promises made at ordination or occasions in which people are designated as caregivers by their communities of faith. Caregivers need to be able to account for their decisions and actions by articulating which sources (Scriptures, practices, doctrine, rulings, and experiences) and norms, or rules of interpretation, they use to support their actions as caregivers. For instance, Sally and her supervisor might cite statements from the Social Principles of United Methodist Church on the rights of the aging.[1] They may also be required by their state's laws to make a report concerning possible elder abuse. These laws may mandate (require) that clergy report instances of elderly neglect to the state's social services.

The primary sources and norms of authority for establishing pastoral care relationships that ensure the well-being of careseekers are the statements outlining governance in religious organizations that designate persons as pastoral caregivers and hold them accountable. These

---

1. In a society that places primary emphasis upon youth, those growing old in years are frequently isolated from the mainstream of social existence. We support social policies that integrate the aging into the life of the total community, including sufficient incomes, increased and nondiscriminatory employment opportunities, educational and service opportunities, and adequate medical care and housing within existing communities. We urge social policies and programs, with emphasis on the unique concerns of older women and ethnic persons, that ensure to the aging the respect and dignity that is their right as senior members of the human community. Further, we urge increased consideration for adequate pension systems by employers, with provisions for the surviving spouse. ("Rights of the Aging," in *The Book of Discipline of The United Methodist Church* (2000), The United Methodist Publishing House, 2000. http://www.umc.org)

include promises concerning religious beliefs and practices made by candidates at ordination or recognition services. These promises become the basic covenant between those designated to offer ministry and the designating organization. For Christians, these beliefs and practices typically concern the meaning of the life, death, and resurrection of Jesus Christ, and the relationship between Jesus Christ, God, and the Holy Spirit. Those designated to provide ministry are accountable for the ways in which their practices reflect their beliefs about the Trinity and the person of Jesus Christ.

Another source and norm of authority is the codes of ethics developed by religious organizations for those designated to provide leadership. Almost all Christian denominations have codes of conduct concerning sexual misconduct, and many also have developed more general codes of conduct, some of which are available online.[2] An example of a code of conduct not only for ordained officers, but also for employees, volunteers, and members, is found in the Standards of Ethical Conduct approved by the 210th General Assembly (1998) Presbyterian Church (U.S.A.) (http://www.pcusa.org/oga/ethics/members.htm). The Standards of Ethical Conduct are summarized here to illustrate the range of issues addressed in a comprehensive code of conduct. The standards for ordained officers begin with these words:

> As an ordained officer in the Presbyterian Church (U.S.A.), in obedience to Jesus Christ, under the authority of Scripture and guided by our Confessions, I affirm the vows made at my ordination, confirm that Jesus Christ is the pattern for my life and ministry and, relying on God's grace, commit myself to the following standards of ethical conduct.
>
> (Professional Code of Ethics, 1998, 3)

---

2. The Disciples of Christ (Christian Church) has a Ministerial Code of Ethics (http://www.homeland.org/Ministers/MinistryGuidelines/ethics.htm). The United Church of Christ has four codes (the Pastor's Code, the Ordained Minister's Code, the Commissioned Minister's Code, and the Licensed Minister's Code), available in the first section of the *Manual on Ministry* (http://www.ucc.org/ministers/manual/index.html). The United States Catholic Conference has codes of ethics for the following organizations: the National Association of Lay Ministry and the National Association of Catholic Campus Ministry Association (http://www.nccbuscc.org). The National Catholic Risk Retention Group has a "Model Code of Pastoral Conduct for Priests, Deacons, Pastoral Ministers, Administrators, Employees, and Volunteers" that can be used as a risk management tool by bishops, pastors, and administrators (http://www.virtus.org/virtuspublications.htm). The Metropolitan Community Church has a code of conduct available to its ministers online at http://www.mccchurch.org. Lutheran, Episcopal, and Methodist pastoral caregivers can seek further guidance on professional conduct from regional offices of their denominations. There are also codes of ethics for pastoral counselors (Ethics for the American Association of Pastoral Counselors: http://www.aapc.edu) and chaplains (The Association for Clinical Pastoral Education: http://www.acpe.edu). The United Methodist Church has no national code of conduct. Clergy need to ascertain whether each annual conference has its own code of conduct.

This document begins by describing how ordained officers are to conduct their lives so as to be "faithful to the gospel and consistent with [their] public ministry" (Professional Code of Ethics, 1998, 3). Such faithfulness is evidenced in spiritual and religious disciplines, honesty, faithfulness (including the honoring of marriage vows), treating people with equal respect, maintaining work, family, health, psychological and spiritual well-being, refraining from exploitative behavior and gossip, and, finally, maintaining an attitude of repentance, humility, and forgiveness.

The document also describes the conduct of ministry within the Presbyterian Church (U.S.A.), including the following:

— Honoring the sacred trust of relationships and maintaining appropriate boundaries
— Being judicious in the exercise of the power and privileges associated with ordination
— Refraining from exploitative behavior, including sexual harassment and misconduct (here there is reference to specific policies on these behaviors)
— Recognizing the need for confidentiality and the limits of confidentiality
— Recognizing the limits of one's expertise and the need for referral

Other sections, while not specifically concerned with pastoral ministry, describe aspects of ministry that can have an impact on such ministry:

— Speaking the truth in love
— Avoiding conflict of interest that compromises one's ministry
— Reflecting one's credentials honestly and giving credit for copyrighted sources
— Refraining from indebtedness that compromises one's ministry
— Fully accounting for funds and properties entrusted to oneself
— Observing limits set by governing bodies on honoraria, etc.
— Accepting the discipline of the church
— Participating in continuing education and professional consultation

The standards also deal with a minister's relationship with congregations from which he or she has left or retired. Ministers who have left a church must, for example, be respectful of the caregiving provided by the current minister, and may not continue caregiving relationships with members unless they are directed to by presbytery and have the consent of their current pastor. A former minister may not, for example, lead the funeral service of a church member without the consent of the current minister.

The final section of these standards for ordained officers is about participation in the ministry of the Church universal by

— being respectful of colleagues in ministry,
— recruiting church members responsibly, and
— cooperating with those working for justice and peace from other faith traditions.

In terms of pastoral care, these three items describe the need for caregivers to respect pastoral caregivers from other traditions and the religious faiths of those seeking care, and the need to work within the interfaith mission of seeking healing and justice that is common to caregivers in many religious traditions.

The Professional Code of Ethics approved by the 201st General Assembly (1998) of the Presbyterian Church (U.S.A.) includes references to the Scripture sources and norms of authority used to develop the code, which reflect the basic norms of the denomination concerning the authority of the Hebrew and Christian Scriptures, as well as the authority of confessional statements. The explicit use of such norms demonstrates the theological foundation of the code.

In what follows, I describe how to establish a contract of care by first considering the limits of confidentiality when careseekers are at risk because they are being neglected or physically, sexually, or psychologically abused. Then I outline other aspects of the basic contract of care of which caregivers must be aware at the outset of any caregiving relationship: sexual harassment and misconduct, dual roles, the limits of professional expertise (i.e., differentiating care from therapy) and the need for referral, and the limits of confidentiality and availability.

Limits of Confidentiality

Pastoral caregivers must always be alert to the need for further assessment when they suspect that a careseeker is experiencing violence or neglect. Physical injuries that are inadequately explained, the use of corporal punishment that leaves physical marks, and signs of inadequate care may be indicators of physical abuse. Caregivers may see indications of neglect when they do a home visit, as Sally Brown did when she visited Louise Haverly. Signs of sexual abuse are more difficult to identify, but caregivers alert to the possibilities of such abuse in a careseeker's story should ask follow-up questions. In chapter 5 I will discuss the assessment of violence, and in chapter 8 what plans of care need to be in place. I now describe how caregivers can ascertain whether their suspicions of abuse need to be assessed by those in social service agencies.

Example

Jeff and Melissa, a married couple who co-led the junior high youth group at St. Andrew's Episcopal Church, noticed a change in Martha, a thirteen-year-old who had been a lively participant in their group activities and discussions. It seemed as though she had changed overnight. She was withdrawn, often staring into space during group discussions and sitting on the sidelines during volleyball games and ping-pong tournaments. At their Saturday afternoon meeting Melissa asked Martha if she would be able to attend the youth retreat, an event she had always enjoyed. Martha hugged herself, stared at the floor, and didn't respond. Melissa suggested that they find a quiet place to talk.

Melissa (1): I'm worried about you, Martha. You've been pretty quiet lately. I've been wondering if something happened at youth group that has upset you.

Martha (1): No, everything here is okay. (She continues to hug herself and begins rocking in her chair.)

Melissa (2): How are things at home?

Martha (2): Okay.

Melissa (3): I know your dad has been looking for a job. Does that make things stressful at home?

Martha (3): No. He and Mom don't seem too worried. (There are a few more minutes of silence.)

Melissa (4): I know something's on your mind, Martha. You may not want to talk about it now, but I want you to know that I'm here for you, I care about you, and I'm ready to listen.

Martha (4): Okay. (She pauses.) You know a few weeks ago when you talked to the girls about going out on dates?

Melissa (5): Yes. We talked about touching, kissing, and how to decide for yourself how close you wanted to be.

Martha (5): Right after that, I went to the movies with Ken Myers. He's in my class at school.

Melissa (6): Was Ken the person with you at the mall a few weeks ago when we bumped into each other?

Martha (6): Yeah. I forgot you met him there.

Melissa (7): Did something happen with Ken?

Martha (7): This is really hard to talk about.

Melissa (8): Yeah, it sounds like it. (There is a pause.)

Martha (8): I feel so ashamed. I should have known not to walk with him in the park at night. I didn't think it would be dangerous. There are usually lots of people around.

Melissa (9): Can you tell me what happened?

Martha (9): Ken wanted to lie down on the grass. We started kissing. Then, all of the sudden, he was trying to unzip my jeans. I told him to stop, but he wouldn't listen. I kind of froze and didn't know what to do. He pinned me down, and said if I yelled he would hit me. Then he had sex with me. (She begins shaking and starts to cry.)

Melissa (10): Oh, Martha, I'm so sorry this happened to you. You must have been so frightened and confused.

Martha (10): After it was over, he acted as if he hadn't done anything wrong. He just stood up and waited for me to get dressed. Then he said that if I told anyone he'd say that I wanted to have sex with him.

Melissa (11): I'm so glad you told me what happened. How are you feeling right now? (Martha and Melissa talk for a while about Martha's feelings of shame and guilt, and her difficulties sleeping and doing school work. Melissa finds out that Martha has avoided Ken, and he has stayed away from her. Then she broaches the subject of talking to others about what has happened.)

Melissa (12): Martha, I'm concerned about your health. It sounds like Ken didn't use a condom.

Martha (12): No. I was scared I might be pregnant, but my

period started last week. But then I started worrying about AIDS. But that couldn't happen to me. It was just once.

Melissa (13): How do you feel about talking to your doctor?

Martha (13): But wouldn't she have to do something, like tell someone else?

Melissa (14): Yes, she would. And I have to do something, too.

Martha (14): What do you mean?

Melissa (15): It's my responsibility as a youth group leader in this church to make a report to the Department of Children and Family Services when I find out that someone like yourself has been hurt. How do you feel about that?

Martha (15): Then my parents would find out. I'm not sure what that would be like. (Melissa and Martha talk about Martha's fears that her mother will blame her for what happened and her father will get angry with Ken. Melissa offers to talk with Martha's parents later that evening and help them understand what has happened. Martha wants Melissa's husband, Jeff, to come so that he can talk to her father. Melissa returns to the issue of filing a report with the Department of Children and Family Services. She expresses concern that Ken be held accountable for his actions, so that what happened to Martha won't happen to someone else. Martha says that he's been hanging out with another young woman in her class and that she is worried about her. She realizes that they need to report what happened. Later that evening, after Melissa and Jeff have met with Martha's parents, Melissa makes a call to her local Department of Children and Family Services, reports what happened, and ascertains what the next steps will be for Martha.)

This case study illustrates the limits of confidentiality regarding careseekers who are vulnerable because they are children, adolescents, elderly, or disabled. Melissa was required by her denomination's code of ethics for volunteer leaders to file a voluntary report to the agency designated in her state's laws on child abuse reporting. Under normal circumstances, pastoral caregivers are required to maintain confidentiality, but if a careseeker is at risk because she is a child, teenager, or vulnerable adult experiencing abuse, or is suicidal, homicidal, psychotic, or experiencing dementia, caregivers must consult with both legal and ecclesial counsel to determine if they must break confidentiality in order to have the risk of harm adequately assessed (Fortune 1988; Bullis 1990). In many states clergy are described as a professional group who are "mandated reporters," a legal term describing who must report suspicions of abuse to local authorities. As a result of the most recent wave of reports of sexual misconduct involving Roman Catholic priests, there is a growing awareness that religious organizations may wittingly or unwittingly use clergy privilege to protect themselves from scandals, including the scandal of clergy pedophiles who prey upon children. The following excerpts from a 2003 report from the National Clearinghouse on Child Abuse and Neglect Information provide information about state laws (http://nccanch.acf.hhs.gov/general/legal/ statutes/clergymandated.cfm):

> Approximately twenty-one States (Arizona, Arkansas, California, Colorado, Connecticut, Illinois, Maine, Massachusetts, Michigan, Minnesota, Mississippi, Missouri, Montana, Nevada, New Hampshire, New Mexico, North Dakota, Oregon, Pennsylvania, Vermont, and West Virginia) currently include members of the clergy among those professionals specifically mandated by those States' reporting laws to report known or suspected instances of child abuse or neglect. In approximately eighteen states (Delaware, Florida, Idaho, Indiana, Kentucky, Maryland, Mississippi, Nebraska, New Hampshire, New Jersey, New Mexico, North Carolina, Oklahoma, Rhode Island, Tennessee, Texas, Utah, and Wyoming) and Puerto Rico, any person who suspects child abuse or neglect is required to report. That broad language appears on its face to include clergy as well as anyone else, but it is possible that the term has been interpreted otherwise.

The following excerpt details the complexities of determining whether pastoral conversations are privileged communications:

> As a doctrine of some faiths, clergy have an obligation to maintain the confidentiality of pastoral communications. Mandatory reporting statutes in some States specify when a communication is privileged. "Privileged communications" is a legal term for the statutory recognition of the right to maintain the confidentiality of communications between certain persons such as professionals and their clients or patients. Privileged communications may be exempt from the reporting laws. The privilege of maintaining this confidentiality under State law must be provided by statute and most States do

provide the privilege in statute, typically in rules of evidence or civil procedure. If the issue of privilege is not addressed in the reporting laws summarized here, it does not mean that privilege is not granted; it may be granted in other parts of State statutes.

This privilege, however, is not absolute. While clergy-penitent privilege is frequently recognized within the reporting laws, it is typically interpreted narrowly in the child abuse or neglect context. The circumstances under which privilege is allowed vary from State to State, and in some States is denied altogether. For example, among States that enumerate clergy as mandated reporters, New Hampshire and West Virginia deny the clergy-penitent privilege in cases of child abuse or neglect.

Detailed information summarizing the child abuse reporting laws of each state is also available from "The Church and Tax Report," a bimonthly publication by Christian Ministry Resources (www.ChurchLawToday .com). In terms of reporting elder abuse, the American Bar Association's Web site (http://www.abanet.org/media/factbooks/eldt1.html) identifies the following states as having laws that designate clergy as mandatory reporters of elder abuse: Alaska, California, Connecticut, Georgia, Missouri, Nevada, Ohio, and Oregon. Given the difficulty of determining whether or not one is a mandated reporter, ministers must consult with their denomination's legal counsel.

For pastoral caregivers, the ethical and legal requirements to report suspicions about abuse can be justified using theological norms, like the norm that the most vulnerable members of society must be protected. Many denominations have made statements condemning violence against children, those with disabilities, and the elderly. Many caregivers use a plan of care (see chapter 8) based upon theological sources and norms of authority in which the first goal is to protect those at risk (Fortune 1983; Cooper-White 1995; Poling 2003).

Disclosures of abuse can occur in unlikely settings. Consider the following example: Lili Park, a female minister, is traveling to a conference with Mi-Ae Cho, a member of the congregation. On their long car journey, Mi-Ae tells her minister about her childhood experiences of being sexually abused by an uncle and notes that this uncle now has children of his own. She says she is worried about one of his daughters, who has stomachaches and nightmares. She wonders if this daughter is being abused. In this illustration, as soon as Lili realized that Mi-Ae might be preparing to describe a child at risk, Lili interrupted Mi-Ae to tell her that she, Lili, might have to inform others who could assess the risk of abuse. Lili needed Mi-Ae to be fully informed about potential limits of confidentiality so that she could make decisions about her disclosures. Lili also needed to consult with legal and ecclesial experts to determine if there is reasonable cause to believe that a child under the age of eighteen years is being abused. When caregivers, like Lili, are familiar with the limits of confidentiality they will establish implicit— and sometimes explicit—contracts with careseekers that ensure their safety and well-being.

Sexual Misconduct

James Donaldson had been the minister at Hope Presbyterian Church for four years. The past year had been challenging for him. An outreach program he had initiated in his second year, which had brought new families into the church, had resulted in conflict between the "old guard" and new members. He was struggling to assimilate these families into the church. He and his wife had become close to a couple who had recently joined the church. They had several family barbeques together, with the children from both families enjoying themselves. They talked about going on a vacation together. When this couple complained to James and his wife about their experiences of the "old-timers" as unfriendly, James in turn described some of his difficulties.

During this time, James felt as though he had lost the focus of his ministry. When he had first started at Hope, he was able to maintain a schedule of exercise, daily prayer, sermon preparation, pastoral visitation, program planning, and meeting preparation that allowed him to be at home some evenings and on his day off. Lately, he was always behind. He tried to squeeze in pastoral visits whenever he could. He had been going into the office on Saturday afternoons to prepare sermon outlines that left him feeling anxious about whether he would be able to connect ideas and flesh out illustrations on his feet in the pulpit. His blood pressure had increased because he no longer exercised with regularity. On the nights he was home he often lingered over dinner, eating and drinking more than he should, because of a sense of unease and emptiness.

In his first years at Hope he had gained a reputation for being a compassionate listener, especially among those who had experienced death. He was often called upon to conduct funeral services of people in the community who had no church affiliation because he took the time to get to know the family in the days after a death and was often able to address the meaning and complexity of death in his sermon and prayers. He knew he was a gifted pastor in this area of ministry and tried to balance this aspect of his ministry with his congregational commitments.

His usual practice, following a funeral service, was to conduct a follow-up visit with those who were in mourning. Lately, he had fallen behind in such visits. One afternoon, after a rancorous encounter in the church kitchen with the chairperson of one of the ladies' auxiliary groups who wanted locks installed on the cabinets, he gave up the idea of working on his sermon and decided to head home early. On the way he stopped, somewhat impulsively, to visit a woman whose husband had died recently. He had remembered her in the middle of the previous night when he was thinking about neglected duties. When he arrived unannounced, she graciously invited him in. He accepted her offer of "something stronger than tea," and with the first sip of a gin and tonic he felt himself relax in a way he hadn't for a long time. As he asked about what the past weeks had been like for her and she tearfully described her sadness and loneliness, he remembered what it was like to feel competent and helpful.

This late-afternoon conversation was the first of many. Over time, he told her about his frustrations with the congregation, and she talked about wanting to date men. He encouraged her, commenting on her attractiveness. During a particularly intense conversation when she described difficulties in her sexual relationship with her deceased husband, he sat beside her and held her. They hugged for a long time before he left that evening. It felt natural for him to comfort her this way.

It is easy to imagine the end of this story. The stage has been set for sexual misconduct to be fully enacted. The minister has lost a spiritual focus, is not able to manage his time, has difficulty controlling compulsive eating and drinking, cannot relieve stress through physical exercise, has been irresponsible in his duties, is burnt out,[3] and, last but not least, has intense needs that are being satisfied in a pastoral caregiving relationship in which he has crossed psychological and sexual boundaries.

The contract of pastoral care must guarantee that caregivers will not engage in sexual or romantic relationships with careseekers. Because of

---

3. Rediger (2003, 38) lists loss of the sense of spiritual disciplines, an undisciplined lifestyle, development of addictions, irresponsibility with professional duties, eroticized behavior, and deterioration of marital relationship as warning signs that the danger of misconduct is imminent.

the power differential between themselves and the caregiver, careseekers cannot give authentic or meaningful consent to such relationships (Fortune 1989). Without this consent, such sexual relations are on the same continuum of coercive sexual relations as sexual abuse and assault. While the desire for sexual contact during an intense pastoral care session may be experienced in the moment as consensual by either or both parties, as Rutter (1989) notes, such relationships are always harmful.

The male minister is often experienced as a father figure: "The parallels to incest with the church 'family' are clear and hold similar devastating consequences" (Cooper-White 1995, 129). When this sacred trust—this "covenantal place of safety and nurture where a parishioner can come with the deepest wounds and vulnerabilities" (Cooper-White 1995, 130)—is broken, the careseeker may feel betrayed by God and lose her religious faith. When such wounds and vulnerabilities include a desire on the part of the careseeker for romantic and/or sexual intimacy, then it is even more important for caregivers to maintain appropriate boundaries. "In order to be truly ministered to by the church's ministers, people must feel free to bring their whole selves, including their vulnerabilities, without fear of violation, exploitation, or re-abuse" (Cooper-White 1995, 130).

Almost all Protestant denominations responded to the wave of clergy sexual scandals in the 1970s and 1980s by establishing sexual misconduct policies defining the terms and outlining procedures for responding to accusations. Caregivers are often now required to sign statements on annual report forms that they have read and are familiar with such policies. The Episcopal Church requires its clergy to attend workshops on sexual misconduct. Knowing the rules, however, may not be enough to prevent some caregivers from crossing sexual boundaries when they are under stress. Caregivers must be able to reflect upon relational dynamics in which their needs become fused with the careseeker's and they feel compelled to use sexual contact to act in overpowering ways. Reflecting upon such dynamics, as I discussed in chapter 2, is not only part of learning how to provide care; it is part of the ongoing work of being a caregiver. Participation in a peer supervision group or in monthly case consultations can provide opportunities for such reflection. Caregivers who find themselves spontaneously engaging in a sexual or romantic interaction with a caregiver must immediately seek supervision.[4] By

---

4. The tendency to act on such desires has increased in the past twenty-five years, says Rediger (2003, 30), because of a shift from an ethics of belief to an ethics of consequences. "This shift tends to make every person his/her own ethical reference point, and often leads to individuals doing whatever 'seems like a good idea at the time.'"

acting upon their desires, they are already ensnared in the web of self-deception that will quickly become more elaborate if they keep their actions secret.

Dual Roles

In the context of providing leadership to communities of faith, caregivers may wear many different hats. They may function as teachers, preachers, worship leaders, caregivers, and committee members. They also inevitably share social moments with church members, including gatherings that may follow worship, wedding receptions, and other celebrative occasions with families in the congregation. Their role as pastoral caregiver must take precedence when, at any point in an interaction, a parishioner raises a pastoral concern.

The dual roles in a pastor's life become problematic when role conflicts occur. An obvious example of such a problem would occur when a minister wishes to date a member of the congregation. She cannot maintain her role as minister of a person and enter a dating relationship with that person. A less obvious example might be a minister in a small town whose sole pharmacist is a church member. What if the minister needs an antidepressant? Will getting his prescription filled at the local pharmacy make it more difficult for the pharmacist to seek care from her minister? A good norm to follow in answering such questions is that the needs of the parishioner come before the pastor's.

Recognizing the Limits of Expertise

All professional codes of ethics for counselors are clear about being mindful of the limits of one's expertise and the need for referral. For example, a psychologist cannot use hypnosis unless she has been trained in this particular form of care and can document such training. Similarly, a minister cannot engage in long-term pastoral counseling unless he has been trained in pastoral counseling, is receiving appropriate supervision, and has clearly negotiated a treatment plan with a care-seeker that includes long-term pastoral counseling.

Pastoral caregivers must not provide care beyond their limits of expertise. When they understand their contract as encompassing crisis counseling and supportive care, they are less likely, in the intensity of a crisis situation, to stray into a psychotherapeutic contract. In order to help caregivers monitor this tendency, I recommend limiting the number of crisis counseling sessions to five or six, to enable caregivers to focus on assessing the crisis and developing the necessary strategies for care, which may include referrals and consultation.

Availability

A final aspect of the contract of care concerns the availability of the caregiver (Denham and Denham 1986, 89). Pastoral caregivers in hospitals and other institutional settings work with clearly articulated expectations about when they are on call. Most pastoral caregivers in churches arrange for colleagues to provide emergency care when they are traveling or on vacation.

Sometimes the nature of a careseeker's crisis makes it necessary for caregivers to describe how they may be contacted outside of their office hours and/or when they will next see the careseeker. With careseekers experiencing acute stress in the aftermath of life-threatening accidents, sudden death, violence, and natural disasters, pastors may need to be explicit about how they can be contacted if, in the days that follow, careseekers need urgent pastoral care. Pastors may also anticipate such needs and arrange for follow-up conversations. In the illustration of a pastoral care conversation between the youth leader, Melissa, and Martha, it would have been appropriate for Melissa to indicate at the end of the visit with Martha and her parents how they could be in touch with her or her husband in the next several days and whether they wanted to schedule a follow-up conversation.

If the nature of the crisis is such that pastors cannot be available around the clock, then they need to say so. Careseekers who are suicidal or in the initial stages of recovery from alcohol or drug addiction need to use hotlines, hospital emergency rooms, and 12-step sponsors. Also, careseekers with mental illnesses that make it difficult for them to regulate intense psychological needs will likely need caregivers with the psychological expertise to judge when emergency care is needed.

As I noted in chapter 3, another issue involving availability concerns providing pastoral care to members of one's former faith community.

Many codes of ethics for pastoral caregivers require ministers to sever pastoral relations when they resign or retire from ministry in a community of faith, and not to make contact with members of such congregations without permission of the current minister.

When pastoral caregivers know the parameters of the contract of care within which pastoral care conversations occur, they are ready for the next step of assessing the extent to which careseekers are dealing with loss, violence, or compulsive ways of coping.

EXERCISE 4: ESTABLISHING THE CONTRACT OF CARE

The purpose of this exercise is to outline the contract of care implicit in your pastoral care conversation by referring to relevant aspects of care identified in (1) this chapter, (2) your denominational code of ethics, and (3) your state laws on child and elder abuse. In order to do this exercise you will need to obtain your denomination's code of ethics for clergy, if there is one. You will also need to locate information about whether clergy are mandated reporters of child and/or elder abuse in your state.

After reviewing all the aspects of the contract described in chapter 4 and your denomination's code of ethics, use the following guidelines to describe in writing which aspects of the contract are important as you establish a contract of care.

— If your careseeker is under the age of eighteen, elderly, and/or disabled, is there a possibility that his or her crisis may involve abuse? Describe what you will do if your careseeker discloses that he or she is at risk.

— Does the careseeker have intense needs for emotional closeness such that she or he may misconstrue the nature of the pastoral care relationship? Identify ways you will maintain appropriate boundaries by not meeting in a private place, not initiating physical contact, and being prepared to talk about physical contact initiated by the careseeker.

— Do you experience desires to have your needs for closeness met in this relationship? Identify how you will guarantee that you do not act on these desires.

— Are there dual conflicting roles? Describe how you will handle such conflict.

— Are there or might there be limits to your expertise in caring for this person? What additional resources might she or he need?
— Is the nature of the crisis such that you need to be explicit about the nature of your availability? If so, what will you say at the conclusion of your next conversation?

5

Psychological Assessment: The Careseeker's Story in Terms of Loss, Violence, and Compulsive Ways of Coping

In my pastoral ministry over the past twenty-five years, I have found that almost all careseekers are dealing with one or more of three issues: loss, violence, and healthy or unhealthy ways of coping with stress.[1] Mourning losses and celebrating gains are dominant themes in the stories of careseekers going through life-cycle transitions like leaving home, becoming married, having children, retiring, experiencing health crises, aging, and facing death. Loss is also a central issue in many crises that bring people into conversation with pastors: the ending of relationships, divorce, managing stepfamily dynamics, unemployment, and living with disabilities, to name a few. Pastors with the skills to assess how careseekers experience loss can be effective in a variety of pastoral care encounters.

A less common but equally urgent theme that surfaces in many careseekers' stories is violence. As pastors become more aware of the frequency and devastating consequences of physical and sexual violence,

---

1. My experiences are reflected in the pastoral care literature from the past twenty years. Mitchell and Anderson's text, *All Our Losses, All Our Griefs: Resources for Pastoral Care*, published in 1983, was the most commonly used text in introductory courses in pastoral care, among a group of pastoral theologians comparing notes at the 1993 Society for Pastoral Theology meeting. An emerging focus of pastoral care at this time was sexual and domestic violence, evidenced in the work of Fortune (1983, 1987), Pellauer, Chester, and Boyajian (1987), Doehring (1987, 1993a, 1993b), Poling (1991), Ramsay (1991), Graham (1992), Imbens and Jonker (1992), Adams (1994), and Cooper-White (1995).

There is a growing interest among pastoral theologians in substance abuse and addictions (Nelson 2004; Dann 2002). This literature is related to a broader theme: how people cope with stress, especially the religious and spiritual ways in which they cope (Pargament 1997).

they are more likely to hear themes of violence and be alert to the urgent need for healing and justice. They must know how to respond when a woman discloses that her partner beats her, a man describes experiences of childhood abuse, or a teenager is a victim of date rape.

A third theme—compulsive ways of coping and addiction—is becoming more common in the stories of careseekers. There is a growing awareness in North America of the effects of compulsive ways of coping—alcoholism, overeating, excessive accumulation of material goods—on the health of persons and families. Pastors are more likely than other professional caregivers to see the effects of compulsive ways of coping because they encounter parishioners with compulsive ways of coping like anorexia or alcoholism in a variety of settings and may visit in their homes. As a result, they are uniquely positioned to name "the elephant in the room" when parishioners are in denial. Besides having the kind of access to people's lives that allows them to identify destructive ways of coping with stress, pastors can help careseekers focus on spiritual and religious coping that satisfies the spiritual cravings underlying compulsive ways of coping.

In this chapter I help pastors to identify and respond to themes of loss, violence, and compulsive ways of coping in the stories of careseekers. I suspect that listening for narrative themes comes more naturally to many pastors than using the diagnostic categories of mental health professionals or the therapeutic frames and strategies of psychotherapists.[2] Working with stories is a dramatically different way of providing care than applying ideas or concepts, like diagnostic categories or models of personality. Many pastoral caregivers will be able to convey a greater sense of presence during a pastoral care conversation when they stay in a narrative mode rather than a conceptual one. While in reality we are always conceptually processing what is happening in the moment, too much conceptualizing can disengage the caregiver from the immediacy of their encounter with the careseeker. Conceptual

---

2. The narrative approach has a long history in pastoral care, going back to one of the founders of the clinical pastoral education movement, Anton Boisen, who in the 1930s taught chaplains to approach patients as "living human documents." Scalise (2003, 197) helpfully sets this often-quoted phrase within a quotation from Boisen that describes the approach to theological education in Boisen's time: "I was much concerned that theological students should have the opportunity to go to first-hand sources for their knowledge of human nature. I wanted them to learn to read human documents as well as books" (Boisen 1936, 10). Gerkin (1986) used this metaphor as the cornerstone of his hermeneutical approach to pastoral care, in which the careseeker's story is set within the horizon of biblical narratives. More recently, Neuger (2001) has developed a narrative approach to counseling with women based on postmodern theories about the social construction of knowledge and, in particular, the therapeutic strategies of White and Epston, used so effectively in Australia with aboriginal clients. Through a process called externalization, the counselor helps the client identify the central problem causing distress and talk about the problem as something external to herself. The client gains a sense of agency in relation to the problem and a new perspective on how the problem relates to family and cultural narratives, especially concerning gender.

frameworks are important later, in reflecting on the conversation, preparing a verbatim, or meeting with a supervisor.

The narrative approach described in this chapter is based upon five assumptions about the stories pastors hear in pastoral care conversations. With these assumptions in mind, pastors can (1) listen more carefully to how parishioners use stories to make sense of their lives and (2) help careseekers coauthor their lives in more deeply meaningful ways.

1. The stories people tell and the ways in which they elaborate themes of loss, violence, and coping behaviors are highly personal and idiosyncratic. This individuality of response makes it necessary to listen for the particularities of people's stories. I am often reminded of the striking ways in which people's stories unfold in unexpected ways when I read novels or see films that portray universal aspects of loss, violence, and compulsive ways of coping. The particular setting (like a New Hampshire winter, an Australian desert, a New Orleans summer), the twists and turns of the plot, and the ways in which characters develop are elements that make each story unique.

Pastors can listen to the unique details of a careseeker's story with the same appreciation for mystery and beauty that they bring to literature and film. They can also recognize the ways in which a careseeker's story sometimes unfolds with the same inevitability as a Shakespearean tragedy when underlying narrative conflicts are not resolved. A pastor, for example, whose personal needs were expressed inappropriately in sexual relationships with parishioners was not able to contemplate retirement, even though his failing health made it difficult for him to fulfill his duties. He remarked with lugubrious humor that he might die in the pulpit and have to be carried out of the church in a final farewell. His lifelong inability to separate his needs from his parishioners' did indeed determine the final chapter of his story, in which he was charged with misconduct and abruptly left the congregation and the ministry.

2. People in crisis tell stories in order to make sense of what has happened to them. They cope with the chaos of intense experiences by organizing them into a narrative sequence. Caregivers can learn much about the careseeker's psychological well-being by simply listening to how the story is told. A person traumatized by life-threatening events will tell fragments of stories, like the flashbacks of the runaway slave, Sethe, detailed in Morrison's (1987) novel *Beloved,* or the disjointed recollections of a battered wife narrated in Doyle's (1996) novel *The*

Woman Who Walked into Doors. When careseekers need to be in control, their stories may be terse, repeated in the same unvarying way after many pastoral care conversations. When their story is fluid, it can have a life of its own, spinning out new meanings during the pastoral care conversation, such that caregiver and careseeker coauthor a continually unfolding story.

3. *The more the careseeker's story can become multilayered and complex enough to encompass the profound experiences of his or her suffering, the more the careseeker will be sustained and even transformed through that suffering.* Conversely, when stories do not allow the full tragedy of suffering to be described, then a careseeker's suffering will be exacerbated. In the novel *The Secret Lives of Bees* (Kidd 2002), fourteen-year-old Lily is obsessed with the story of her mother, who was killed when Lily was four. Lily knew only the briefest details of this death; her father told her that she had come between her parents when they were arguing, picked up a gun lying on the floor, and pulled the trigger, accidentally killing her mother. Everyone in her South Carolina farming community knew the story of this death, but no one spoke of it. Lily's profound longing for her mother and insatiable need to know her mother's story propels her to run away from home. She instinctively finds the place that holds the secrets of her mother's life: the Black Madonna Honey Farm, run by three black women, the Boatwright sisters. Lily finds out that her mother, deeply depressed, left her in her father's care when she was four and came to live at the Honey Farm. The story of her mother's complete devotion to her, which she has told herself over and over, is shattered. All she can think about now is that her mother left her. "Knowing can be a curse on a person's life. I'd traded in a pack of lies for a pack of truth, and I didn't know which was heavier. Which one took the most strength to carry around? It was a ridiculous question, though, because once you know the truth, you can't ever go back and pick up your suitcase of lies" (Kidd 2002, 256). Eventually the truth sets her free when she is able to mourn for her mother, drawing upon the rituals of the Daughters of Mary, an eclectic circle formed by the Boatwright sisters.

4. *The deeper the loss and the more life-threatening the violence, the less likely people will be able to return to the way their life was before the crisis. The stories they construct describing their past, present, and future will be irrevocably changed.* Suffering is often not an experience from which people "recover," such that they simply go back to the way they were living before their experience of suffering. Grieving is not about "get-

ting over" the loss of a significant other; rather, it is about finding new ways to be spiritually connected, and these new ways involve a reconstruction of the stories and practices that represent who the griever and the grieved are.

5. *These stories are shaped by the stories they have heard in their families, communities, and culture,[3] which may help them understand and cope with their suffering or make it worse.* Constructing and reconstructing one's story is not done in isolation from others or from the meaning systems of one's family, communities, and culture. Given that persons are embedded in social networks and, as pastoral caregivers believe, spiritual networks involving transcendent realities, the reconstruction of meaning does not simply involve a single person. The stories told within our family, our community, and our culture have the power to keep us mired hopelessly in suffering without purpose or meaning. This is what happens to women of faith whose pastors tell them that if they pray hard enough, they will prevail against husbands who physically abuse them. They appeal to the story of Jesus on the cross, drawing a parallel with the cross that these women must bear, to save their husbands and keep their marriages together. Conversely, the stories of families and communities have the power to bind up the wounds of the brokenhearted and liberate slaves from captivity. Consider, for example, the stories told by people attending a meeting of Alcoholics Anonymous, about their struggles to maintain sobriety or their efforts to make amends with those they have harmed. These stories can sustain the participants, helping them make it through the next twenty-four hours without a drink.

These five assumptions, concerning (1) the idiosyncratic nature of stories about suffering, (2) the way stories help people construct meaning, (3) the way stories can help or hinder healing, (4) the need to reconstruct meanings when life events irrevocably change people, and (5) the role of the family, community, and culture in constructing stories that can imprison or liberate, are part of a "constructivist" psychological approach to understanding grief (Neimeyer 1995, 2000, 2001). This approach is used throughout the ensuing discussion of losses, violence, and compulsive ways of coping.

Before embarking on this discussion, we must distinguish between

---

3. The careseeker's narrative "has many strands within it, even potentially contradictory strands, that are held together by foundational interpretive assumptions. These assumptions, story lines, and plots are generated through personal experiences, familial roles and stories, institutional influences, and larger cultural themes. They are woven by an individual into a personal history that makes meaning out of the past, sense out of the present, and direction out of the future" (Neuger 2001, 43).

constructivist and social constructionist perspectives. Constructivist psychologists highlight the capacity of individuals to construct idiosyncratic meanings out of suffering. Social constructionist psychologists highlight the ways in which meanings are socially constructed. While the two perspectives may seem at odds with each other, when combined they allow caregivers to look at a careseeker's meaning systems from two angles, similar to looking at the well-known optical illusion depicting two faces in profile facing each other or a white vase set against a dark background. Another way of describing the differences between the two perspectives is that constructivist psychologists are interested in the fingerprints: the idiosyncratic imprint left when a particular person interacts with his or her context. The constructionist is interested in the person and context as a fluid process of meaning-making in which one can hardly distinguish between the person as an entity separate from his or her context. In this chapter, I focus on the idiosyncratic meanings constructed by individuals; in the next I consider the role of family, community, and culture in ameliorating or exacerbating the suffering of a careseeker. Both perspectives are necessary in order for caregivers to appreciate (1) how people's stories are shaped but not wholly determined by the narratives of family, community, and culture, and (2) the agency of individuals to make meaning in remarkably unique ways.

Loss

Loss is the most common source of human suffering. Consider the gains and losses of puberty, leaving home, beginning a partnered relationship, or choosing to be single. Even a celebratory transition such as marriage involves losses (Anderson and Fite 1994), in that making a final choice for a partner means closing down other options. In addition, younger adults getting married may be leaving home physically and psychologically. Yet these various losses are often denied or satirized in cultures that idealize romantic love. When a person going through an anticipated life cycle transition, like becoming married, or an unexpected crisis like divorce does not have enough social support from a partner, family, and friends, she can become overwhelmed by the losses that come with a transition or crisis. She may turn to her minister for help. If a pastor's ministry includes keeping in contact with parishioners going through life cycle transitions or in crisis, then he or she may be able to provide a sustaining presence.

The Phases of Grief

The first thing a caregiver can do is to assess the stage of grief the care-seeker is in: the acute stage in which feelings are intense and chaotic or the long-term phase of coming to terms with the loss through a process of meaning-making. The first assessment question to ask when someone seeks care because of a loss is what phase of grief he or she is experiencing: acute or long-term. If the loss has just occurred, she will be in the acute phase of grief, with all of its intense dynamics. In contrast, a person who is struggling with questions about the meaning of a past loss and is not experiencing the intense dynamics of the acute phase of grief is likely to be in the long-term phase of grief. The complexity in assessing the phase of grief is that some people may not be able to express the range and intensity of feelings that are part of the acute phase of grief because of family or cultural rules prohibiting the expression of such feelings. They may appear to be in the long-term process of coming to terms with loss, without having experienced the full psychological and spiritual impact of the loss, which hits people in the acute stage of grief. Lily, the protagonist in *The Secret Lives of Bees* (Kidd 2002), for example, was a fourteen-year-old who, for all appearances, had "gotten over" her mother's death, which had occurred when she was four. No one except Rosaleen, the housekeeper who knew her better than anyone else, suspected that Lily's inner life was a never-ending lament for her dead mother. It was only after Lily knew the whole story of her mother that she could fully experience the rage at the heart of her grief and begin the long-term process of coming to terms with her mother's death.

In the acute phase of grief, people experience the immediacy of their loss, the sense of the unreality of this loss, and the disorganizing effects of grief. They may feel alternatively numb and reimmersed in the intensity of grief. Physiological symptoms like sleeplessness and loss of appetite may correspond to their psychological and spiritual pain, like their denial of the loss, their sense of chaos, and their numbness. In the midst of this chaos may come sharp feelings—anger, intense sadness, and guilt—as loss is experienced over and over again, sometimes as if it were the first.

When someone is in the acute phase of grief, caregivers need to ask questions first about his or her safety and must evaluate the possibility of suicide. (While treatment planning will be discussed more fully in chapter 8, I make note of treatment issues throughout this chapter.)

Caregivers should assess whether the loss is so severe that the careseeker may feel that life is no longer worth living. This can happen when a romantic or marital relationships ends, in an extreme financial crisis, or when someone is accused of a highly shameful crime.

Another treatment issue that is of immediate concern in the acute phase of grief is helping people learn to manage their intense psychological reactions. In the immediate aftermath of the loss, the pastor can have weekly conversations in which parishioners can chronicle the "crazy" aspects of grief, like momentarily "forgetting" that loss has occurred—a death, a diagnosis of cancer, a recently acquired disability. Through empathic listening the pastor can convey a nonanxious acceptance of her parishioner's experience of acute grief. The parishioner can learn to regulate the intensity of her feelings by remembering her pastor's calm response.

One of the unique ways pastoral caregivers can provide care in the acute phase of grief is helping careseekers find religious and spiritual practices that connect them with God and a sense of the sacred. Taking inventory of what practices have helped in the past can prompt a parishioner to be more intentional in her spiritual practices. Does she pray? When? Does she simply talk to God about what she feels? Does she ask for help? If so, what kind of help? Does she read the Bible? If so, what passages? Does she listen to music that is spiritually uplifting? Does she engage in activities that connect her with nature and the beauty of creation? Has she ever kept a journal when she needs to reflect upon intense psychological responses to loss? Her answers will indicate whether she is able to connect with God, or if the crisis has left her bereft of spiritual ways of coping.

There are a variety of complicating factors in grief. Some contextual factors make grief more complex: the type of death, for example, sudden, unexpected, violent, and mutilating death; the death of a child; and death after a long illness (Karaban 2000). Other factors have to do with spiritual and psychological limitations within those psychologically responding to loss. For example, a person with a tendency to abuse alcohol under stress will numb intense feelings with alcohol, never fully experiencing his or her psychological response to loss. A person who has a tendency to become psychotic under stress may create a paranoid inner world as a way of coping with grief. One's community and culture may also be a resource or roadblock (see chapter 7). Many middle- and upper-class Euro-American cultures and religious traditions, for example, discourage mourners from intense expressions of public grief after the religious rites following the death are observed. A Caribbean American culture, in contrast, may allow a more extended and expressive time for grief to unfold and have religious rites that support the waves of grief that may come within the first year following a death.

In this chapter and the next, we review an assessment process that takes into account the psychological, familial, religious, and cultural resources and roadblocks that will either help grief unfold in graceful ways or block grief. By using this psycho-spiritual-social perspective, caregivers can develop plans of care that seek the full expression of grief, not only among individuals, but also among families, communities, and cultures. The more people can fully mourn their losses, the more they can redeem their suffering through the construction of complex meanings that can bear the full weight of their suffering.

Typically, the chaos of the acute phase of grief will begin to subside over time, making it easier to regulate the intense feelings and reactions of grief. The duration of the acute phase of grief is individual and contextual. When adequate time, support, and resources allow acute grief gradually to subside, mourners become ready for the long-term process of reconstructing their lives, including their relationships with the people, places, or things that have been lost. When loss involves death, for example, Van Katwyk (1993) describes this reconstruction process as the ongoing reconstruction of the stories of

— who the dead person is to the mourners,
— who the mourners are as people who have lived through this death, and
— who God is to those in mourning.

This reconstruction of stories involves "transforming the spiritual and vocational identity of the family" as the person who has died is incorporated into who this family is and who God is to this family (Van Katwyk 1993, 146). This reconstruction of narrative is played out in the reconstruction of personal, family, and religious practices, for example, practices that have to do with reconnecting with the person who is dead in the midst of the ongoing life of the family and community.

Van Katwyk's emphasis on the need for reconstructing stories and relationships in the midst of grief is also made by constructivist psychologists (Attig 2000; Klass 2002; Neimeyer 2001). Neimeyer, for example, highlights the need for new models of grief that draw upon current theories of psychological constructivism, intersubjective psychology, and multicultural and contextual approaches to psychology. These constructivist psychologists go beyond a psychological model that emphasizes psychological disengagement and acceptance of ultimate separation (Hagman 2002) and offer a psychospiritual model that emphasizes maintaining connections with what has been lost. While few of them draw upon theological perspectives in the ways Van Katwyk (1993) does, some encourage people in grief to seek religious meanings about loss, death, and life after death as a means of spiritually connecting with what has been lost and those who have died, and to use religious and spiritual practices that strengthen these connections.

Types of Loss

Assessing loss also requires understanding the type of loss people are experiencing. There are six general categories of loss: material, relationship, intrapsychic, functional, role, or systemic losses (Mitchell and Anderson 1983). As the following discussion will illustrate, many of these types of loss overlap.

1. *Material losses* are extrinsic, that is, they involve losing assets. An example might be losing money in stocks designated for retirement. Besides having extrinsic value, many material losses also have intrinsic value, i.e., personal meaning that connects people psychologically or spiritually with times, places, or persons who are highly significant (Mitchell and Anderson 1983). For example, a man may become upset when he realizes that he has lost the gold chain and cross that were given to him at his first communion service by his godmother. The cross has intrinsic value to him. A material loss can include a disabled person's lack of physical access to a place or building, like a church, that may have great sacred and/or aesthetic meaning. Similarly, a geographical move may involve the loss of access to highly valued activities and places. If a crisis is related to a new physical or mental disability that restricts or blocks access to valued places, material losses can be enormous.

In assessing whether a careseeker is responding to a material loss, caregivers should ask whether a crisis or transition has a financial impact and/or involves the loss of objects or even places that have intrinsic and even sacred value in that the object refers to a transcendent reality (Pargament and Mahoney 2002).

2. *Relational loss* is the ending of possibilities for intimacy: physical, psychological, intellectual, aesthetic, recreational, spiritual, and sexual. Divorce has to do primarily with relational loss. Divorced spouses expe-

rience the loss of the various ways in which they were close to each other as husband and wife. They may be able to retain a working relationship as parents that occasionally brings them close to each other. Children experience the relational losses of having parents in separate households. Death is the most profound example of relationship loss because there is no further opportunity to have contact with a person through one's senses (seeing, hearing, touching, and smelling the significant other). The loss of physical interaction can be experienced as an ultimate separation from the person who has died. Illness that includes dementia, like Alzheimer's, involves relational losses for caregivers that are as profound as death.

3. *Intrapsychic loss* has to do with the loss of a symbol or ideal that may be associated with persons, places, and things that play an important role within a person's inner world. The ending of a pregnancy, for example, can include the loss of whatever images were formed of the child-to-be. The loss is of a "dream child" that exists within the pregnant woman's inner world. The more vividly this dream child was imagined, the greater will be the immediate sense of loss. Intrapsychic loss can occur when a relational loss reveals something that destroys an ideal. When the death of a spouse uncovers infidelity or financial mismanagement, then the symbol of the spouse as faithful is broken.

4. *Functional loss* involves the loss of some function of the body. This type of loss is related to physical disability due to age, illness, or disease. It often involves the very difficult shift from independence to dependence on others, as well as the intrapsychic losses that accompany no longer being self-sufficient and in charge of one's own life. For example, a woman who has been athletic all of her life injures her knee and loses her routine of physical exercise. Exercise helped her deal with the stress she carried in her body and offset a tendency toward depression. The more physically fit she was, the greater her sense of self-agency. With the loss of her exercise routine, she experiences the intrapsychic loss of an image of herself as strong and capable.

5. *Role loss* involves the loss of a particular role, like the role of daughter, teacher, therapist, or minister, and often accompanies transitions like death, graduation, promotion, retirement, or other job changes. When one's primary connection to another is based upon a contract or agreement, it is important to acknowledge fully that the completion of the contract ends the relationship. When, for example, a therapeutic relationship ends, there can be no possibility of another kind of relationship beginning. Similarly, when a minister leaves a

congregation, she no longer functions as pastor to any member. When there has been a long pastorate and it feels like the minister has become part of the family, it can be difficult to accept the finality of the ending of the contractual relationship.

6. *Systemic losses* involve changes in family systems, communities of faith, and other organizations. What is lost is the particular way in which a system functions. When a congregational system changes and no longer functions in the same way, members may experience systemic loss. A small rural congregation, for example, functioned as an extended family until there was an influx of members from a large housing development. The leadership initiated programming to meet the needs of these young working parents. Longtime members complained that the pastor didn't do as much visitation as before. The women's auxiliary group didn't understand why the younger women weren't interested in their group, and instead wanted to form a morning book club that included child care. Long-term members were reacting to systemic change—the loss of their church as an extended family in which the minister functioned as a chaplain and newcomers fit into family traditions.

Systemic change can occur when the persons significant in shaping a system depart. An extended family gathers every year to celebrate the birthday of its aging matriarch. When she dies, this gathering may end, and this configuration of the family system may no longer exist. In training and educational organizations, a class of students or interns often shapes the organizational system in ways that are unique from one year to the next. For example, in one year there may be some class comedians that bring a certain level of hilarity to the whole organization. Members of the ongoing training staff may experience the systemic loss of a certain formality and seriousness. Others may enjoy the new role of humor, and regret the return of a more somber atmosphere when the interns depart.

Systemic loss occurs in families when people become engaged or married and a new family system is formed as the fiancé or spouse enters the family (Anderson and Fite 1994). When a son or daughter leaves home, the family system also shifts as the independence of the departing member is acknowledged and new relational configurations are formed with those left behind (Anderson and Mitchell 1993). When a family involved in the leadership of a religious community departs, the community has to mourn the passing of the church system that included this leadership. A new organizational system emerges once the leadership changes.

In assessing the psychological responses to loss that may be part of a careseeker's crisis, caregivers can also listen for multiple types of losses. The more types of losses—material, relational, intrapsychic, functional, role, systemic—a person experiences, the more complicated his or her grief will be. A frail elderly person who breaks her hip and has to move into a nursing home is dealing with the material loss of her home, the functional loss of mobility, the role of homemaker, and many intrapsychic losses. If she is a member of the church that was just described, she may feel like she is also losing her church home. In assessing types of loss, it is helpful to note whether the person in grief is going through a life-cycle transition, because certain losses are associated with various life cycles. For example, midlife crises may be triggered by a functional loss, like a knee injury, that represents intrapsychically—that is, in the inner world—the losses associated with aging. Recognizing a careseeker's life-cycle transition can make it easier for pastoral caregivers to understand and respond to the various losses. To complicate matters, several life-cycle transitions can occur simultaneously, making it more difficult to identify the losses associated with each transition. For example, a young adult may graduate from school, leave home, and become married within a short period of time. The pastor doing premarital counseling, aware that this young couple seems overwhelmed by their new life, can help them sort through the losses and gains involved in each of these transitions.

Pastoral caregivers assessing the ways in which life-cycle transitions and types of loss interact may find it helpful to use the chart below, that lists the life-cycle transitions on a horizontal axis and the types of losses on a vertical axis. In the example of the young adults just described, a caregiver would complete the chart.

	Graduating	Leaving Home	Becoming Married
Material Loss			
Relational Loss			
Intrapsychic Loss			
Role Loss			
Systemic Loss			

Assessing Loss

Within each box the caregiver can note details about how a type of loss or gain may be part of each life-cycle transition. For example, leaving home may involve material loss if one's parents are no longer paying for financial expenses. Graduation involves role loss; the young person is no longer in the role of student and now assumes whatever role comes with the work he or she does. Students who have been part of professional education programs may have had the opportunity at intern sites to "try on" a new professional role. Students graduating from more academically oriented educational programs may find the transition from student to a work-related role more difficult. The young single adult who becomes married at the same time that she graduates and leaves home may experience a high degree of stress. She is thrust into a fully "adult" identity. Stress may manifest itself in premarital numbness and emotional disengagement or hyperactivity, with obsessive attention to the minute details of the wedding. Charting of the interacting transitions/crises and types of loss will help a caregiver gain an overview of the complexity of her grief. The acute responses to grief can be addressed by creating space for people in crisis to experience the intensity of their feelings, reflect upon them, and find strategies that allow for mourning losses.

The long-term process of reconstructing one's story can be part of ongoing pastoral care. In the case of the young adult described above, this is the process of *becoming* married, as Anderson and Fite (1994) note. When existential/spiritual/religious/sacred dimensions are part of the process and are a subtheme in the reconstruction of her story, she may experience a deep sense of trust, hope, and love in her relationships with God, others, and self.

Violence

A second frame that can be used by a caregiver listening to a careseeker's story has to do with violence: the use of physical, psychological, and sexual ways to overpower or have power over another. In order to use this frame to understand a careseeker's story, caregivers need to be able to identify the various forms that violence can take. Within families, violence can be physical, psychological, sexual, and can also take the form of neglect. Violence can occur between domestic partners, parents and children, elderly and younger generations, and among siblings. Violence occurring outside of the family can take similar forms, like sexual or physical assault by strangers, bullying, hazing, and robbery. Trauma may also result from life-threatening events, like being in an accident or natural disaster, and life in the workplace for police officers, fire fighters, emergency personnel, and medical teams.[4]

The life-threatening quality of violence may involve actual physical threat to one's life and/or the violation of one's basic sense of self, as occurs with sexual assault and abuse. The psychological response to violence, called trauma, is determined by the life-threatening nature of the violence. Trauma may, in turn, lead to acute stress disorder (American Psychological Association 2000), which occurs within four weeks of the traumatic event and may last a few days, or as long as four weeks. These three responses to the life-threatening stressor all occur and often alternate:

— *Numbing:* Numbness and emotional detachment from the violent event, a lack of awareness of what is going on around him or her (like being in a daze), and difficulty remembering details of the event

— *Avoidance:* Avoidance of anything that reminds the victim of what has happened

— *Intrusion:* Reexperiencing the violent event through recurring dreams, flashbacks, intrusive thoughts, often triggered by a smell, sensation, sound, or something associated with the violence

These responses actually increase anxiety, as the victim's neurological "alarm system" seems to become too highly sensitive. In acute stress disorder, these responses disrupt the victim's social, occupational, and relational functioning.[5]

Trauma may also lead to posttraumatic stress disorder (PTSD), a more severe psychological response to violent events. Both PTSD and acute stress disorder are psychological responses to a life-threatening event, and both feature an alternation between (1) reexperiencing the traumatic event and (2) avoidance of and emotional disconnection from anything associated with the violent event. The severity of the traumatic stressor most often determines whether or not people experience PTSD. With PTSD, the avoidance and numbness act on a more global basis regarding the victim's estrangement from others, emotional disengagement, and dread about the future.

4. Car accidents are "probably the single most common form of trauma that causes PTSD," note Weaver, Flannelly, and Preston (2003, 50).

5. Some people have a resilient response to traumatic stressors, with little or no loss of functioning (Bonanno 2004).

The defining feature of PTSD is that it lasts longer than four weeks, indicating that the level of stress was such that healthy ways of coping were not sufficient in alleviating the acute stress response. The acute phase of PTSD is less than three months. In the chronic phase, which begins after three months, the "emergency" ways of dealing with the trauma become a way of life. PTSD can have a delayed onset in which the responses to trauma are not experienced until at least six months after the event.

Given the extent to which trauma as the psychological response to violence is determined by the life-threatening nature of that violence, it is important to examine more closely the role of power in the experience of violence. As discussed in chapter 1, power dynamics, as a feature of relationships, can take the form of mutual empowerment, overpowering others, and being overpowered. In cultures in which violence is common to many types of relationships, the word "power" may take on a singular meaning: having power over others. Violence involves using aspects of a relationship—physical, psychological, and sexual interactions, and interactions to do with providing care—to have power over another in the form of physical, psychological, and sexual violence, as well as neglect.[6]

Violence can occur in any relationship. Between adults, it can happen in dating and long-term relationships, within gay or heterosexual couples. It can occur among adult siblings in a family, between acquaintances or strangers, and in relationships involving a power differential determined by roles (a caregiver and careseeker, therapist and client, and so on). Violence can also happen between an adult and a child, a teenager, or another adult who is vulnerable because of particular disabilities. It can happen between an adult and younger sibling or stepsibling. It can happen between a stranger and a child, teen, or vulnerable adult. Among children and teens, violence can occur among siblings and stepsiblings, in bullying relationships, dating relationships, acquaintances, gangs, and in hazing or so-called initiation rites.

Violence is often a reoccurring pattern in relationships and in family, community, and cultural systems. It's not uncommon to find intergenerational patterns of violence within a person's genogram, patterns that may well coexist with community and cultural patterns of violence. For this reason, caregivers need to determine if violence is also occur-

---

6. Fortune and Poling (1995) include another type of violence: the destruction of property and pets. The threat of using the same physical force on a person becomes a way of having power over that person.

ring in any of the relational systems of the careseeker. This "taking stock" can be a shocking experience of discovering a hitherto hidden underside of violence that spreads like a cancer among all of the careseeker's relational matrix. Alert to the violence in the careseeker's life, the caregiver may also become more acutely aware of the underside of violence that may be part of his or her own life. Monitoring how one's own story resonates with a victim's story (see chapter 2) becomes a key aspect of caring for victims of violence.

Relational patterns in which violence is used as a way of dealing with conflict need to be assessed. In a cycle of violence, internal feelings of helplessness increase under stress, often leading to interpersonal conflict that escalates until there is a trigger event—an event that becomes the trigger for violence. In the novel *The Woman Who Walked into Doors*, Paula vividly remembers the first time her husband hit her. "I wouldn't do what he wanted, he was in his moods, I was being smart, he hated me being pregnant, I wasn't his little Paula anymore—and he drew his fist back and he hit me" (Doyle 1996, 163). She vividly recalls what immediately preceded the punch: "I said, Make your own . . . tea. That was what happened. Exactly what happened. I provoked him. I always provoked him" (Doyle 1996, 163). At a superficial level, Paula thought her husband hit her simply because she wouldn't fulfill a wifely duty; at a deeper level she knew that he felt overpowered by her and her pregnancy.

If people in conflict have no healthy ways of coping with escalating conflict, then they will respond to a trigger event by acting in violent ways that were modeled to them in formative experiences. After the explosion of the abuse, there may be intense remorse, or denial and emotional shutdown. Without professional intervention, the cycle usually continues and escalates. The cycle, first described by Lenore Walker (1979), includes the following phases:

1. The person at risk of becoming violent feels overpowered psychologically at work and/or at home. The need for control intensifies, and he or she lacks psychological resources to regulate intense feelings. When there is interpersonal conflict, his or her sense of helplessness increases.
2. If he or she doesn't have healthy ways of coping with (1) an increased sense of helplessness, (2) a desire to overpower, and (3) the interpersonal conflict, he or she will respond to a trigger event with an act of violence.

3. In the act of violence he or she uses sexual, physical, or psychological means to overpower the other, or may neglect to care for a child or elder in ways that put the victim in immediate risk.

4. Afterwards he or she may feel remorseful, apologizing for what he or she has done and pleading for forgiveness, or he or she may deny the violence, naming physical abuse as discipline or sexual contact as "sex education" or "just affectionate touching" or "horsing around."

The next time the perpetrator experiences helplessness and interpersonal conflict, the cycle will recur because violence is effective in ending the power struggle, at least temporarily. Without outside intervention, the cycle of violence is likely to escalate.

Pastoral caregivers must be alert to the possibility of violence and ask questions in order to determine if violence is part of a crisis. When a couple is experiencing conflict, the careseeker can ask how anger is expressed and what typically happens when they get into an argument. If there is any indication of physical abuse—suspicious injuries, intense anxiety, rage, or a need for control—then the careseeker should speak with the possible victim separately. Any references to violence—like the destruction of property or pets, threats, shoving—should be followed with specific questions about the use of physical force.

A caregiver should consider the possibility of abuse when a child, teenager, or elderly person (1) has suspicious injuries, (2) has run away from home, (3) has behavioral problems at church, home, or school, (4) has intense anxiety, or (5) shows signs of being neglected. Children or teenagers need to be questioned about whether there is conflict at home with any family member, how conflict is handled, whether and how they are disciplined, and whether they are ever touched in ways that make them feel uncomfortable. They can also be questioned about possible violence outside of the home in the form of bullying, sexual harassment, and sexual abuse or assault. Caregivers can ask elderly persons about the care they receive and whether they ever feel physically threatened or uncomfortable with physical contact.

If there is any indication of violence, then caregivers must ensure the safety of the victim. In terms of child or elder abuse, caregivers need to ascertain whether they are mandated reporters (see chapter 4). When there is domestic violence, the caregiver must make sure that the victim knows how to get help by calling a hotline or the police, or going to a shelter (see chapter 8).

Once physical safety is assured, pastoral caregivers can help victims establish a sense of psychological safety by assessing the extent to which victims are reexperiencing memories in nightmares, anxiety attacks, or flashbacks, and how they cope with these experiences. Are they able to calm themselves by doing deep breathing or other relaxation techniques? Can they seek an inner space in which they can regain a sense of safety and equilibrium? If they are not able to manage these intrusive symptoms of trauma, then pastoral caregivers need to refer them to mental health professionals. It is not appropriate for pastors to provide care to victims who do not know how to manage the reexperiencing of violence because pastoral conversations about the victims' experiences can intensify anxiety, flashbacks, and nightmares, and make their suffering worse.

Many of the strategies that victims learn in counseling help them psychologically center themselves amidst the storm of reexperiencing violence. Pastoral counselors can supplement the coping strategies used by victims by exploring whether they find it helpful to draw upon spiritual or religious practices. For example, victims may want to focus on a religious or spiritual image or thought when they are calming themselves. One victim said the phrase "The Lord is my shepherd" while she inhaled during relaxation exercises, and "I shall not want" when she exhaled. These phrases helped her reexperience a sense of trust in the world. Another victim visualized a stained-glass window in her place of worship depicting Jesus comforting children. In such visualization she remembered what it was like to be in a place she experienced as sacred and to feel comforted. A man recalled an image from the prophet Jeremiah, of a tree whose roots reach far down into parched soil for water; a tree that is not uprooted by strong winds and can still draw sustenance. During relaxation exercises, he imagined drawing strength from the ground through his body. These victims found ways of drawing upon their religious faith and spirituality in using meditation and other relaxation techniques to cope with intrusive memories, flashbacks, and feelings.

In exploring the use of spiritual or religious practices, pastoral counselors and victims need to evaluate their effectiveness in lowering anxiety and alleviating the numbness and emotional disengagement that can come in the aftermath of violence. For example, one victim initially recited the Lord's Prayer when she felt anxious. She soon realized that, at this point in her recovery, images of God as Father were not comforting because of her experiences with men who had abused their power. When she focused instead on praying to Jesus, she felt a genuine sense of comfort and safety.

In order for victims to explore and reflect upon the effect of their spiritual and religious practices, they need to trust caregivers not to impose religious and spiritual practices and meanings upon them. Empowering victims is an essential ingredient of pastoral care. Victims who have grown up in faith communities where they were told what to believe and how to practice their faith may cast the pastoral caregiver in the role of God's spokesperson, wanting him or her to tell them how to pray. The more victims can learn to recognize and share with their caregiver what it is like when they draw upon their religious faith and spiritual practices, the more they will be able to construct religious meanings and spiritual practices that are personally relevant and enhance a sense of their self-agency: their ability to be in charge of their lives. Pastoral care entails the establishment of a trusting relationship in which victims can fully explore their spiritual and religious practices and their underlying beliefs. Being able to trust their pastoral counselor is a part of establishing a sense of safety in the initial phase of pastoral care. Without such a relationship, victims cannot engage in the long-term work of finding religious and spiritual meanings to their suffering (chapter 7).

A final area of violence assessment concerns the risk of suicide. In assessing the risk of suicide, caregivers can keep in mind certain risk factors. Pretzell (in Hunter 1990, 1235) lists high stress factors among those who are suicidal: low personal resources, stress associated with social oppression (i.e., a gay or lesbian teenager dealing with high school homophobia and harassment; college students going through hazing), recent loss, physical illness, physical isolation, and the use of alcohol. Pretzel suggests also checking out stress, symptoms, support systems, lifestyle, communications with significant others, and medical status. White males constitute 70 percent of all suicides in the United States, and the suicide rate among older white men is at least twice that of younger men. "Since white males in general enjoy greater socioeconomic status than all other groups, they appear to suffer more from the fall in social status in old age" (Hoff 1989, 177). Higher rates of suicide among young Native American and urban blacks than white young people suggest a correlation between poverty, racism, and suicide. Some research on women (Hoff 1989, 177) has linked conflict and abuse in intimate relationships with suicide attempts and suicide.

In assessing the risk of suicide or homicide in the midst of a crisis conversation, you may deliberately ask whether the person in crisis has thoughts about ending her or his life or even killing someone with whom she or he is very angry. Asking such questions will not "plant the idea" in a careseeker's head. Instead, such questions often bring a sense of relief to careseekers, giving them permission to share their suicidal or homicidal thoughts with a caregiver. If persons seeking care describe such thoughts, it is important to immediately ask the following series of questions:

— how often and when they have these thoughts about ending their lives or harming another person
— whether family members or friends have attempted or committed suicide
— whether they have attempted to commit suicide in the past
— whether they have imagined how they would kill themselves
— whether they have a plan, and the means to carry out a plan[7]

If a careseeker reports having frequent thoughts of ending her life, has not attempted to commit suicide before, does not have a plan or the means to carry it out, then the caregiver can refer him or her to counseling. If a careseeker responds in the affirmative to all of the assessment questions, then pastoral caregivers must immediately accompany the careseeker to an emergency room for evaluation.

Substance Abuse, Addiction, Compulsive Ways of Coping

A third frame to use in assessing a careseeker's crisis is how he or she copes with stress. Harmful ways of coping may involve compulsive behaviors such as overworking, overeating, overexercising, anorexia, substance abuse and addiction, excessive shopping, obsessive gambling, cutting oneself, and compulsive sexual behaviors, like excessive masturbation or use of Internet pornography. Clearly some of these forms of compulsive behaviors distort aspects of a healthy life—work, eating, exercise, and sexual pleasure—that become harmful when practiced compulsively; that is, when people experience an irresistible impulse to engage in the activity, regardless of the rationality of the motivation. Substance addiction can be distinguished from other forms of compulsive behavior in that it involves a chemical dependency and a genetic predisposition for the formation of such a dependency. For this reason,

---

7. "The more specific, deadly, and available the means are, the higher the risk will be. . . . The use of pills is the most common means of suicide in the U.S., with guns the second most common" (Pretzell, in Hunter 1990, 1235).

I use the term addiction, not compulsive behavior, to refer to chemical dependency, and I discuss assessment of addictions after describing how caregivers can assess compulsive ways of coping.

For several reasons pastoral caregivers may have difficulty knowing the extent of a person's compulsive ways of coping. First, such behaviors are usually kept private, especially when they are experienced as shameful. Second, cultural attitudes that normalize compulsive behaviors can impede the assessment. Among college students, for example, binge drinking is seen as an acceptable way to socialize and have fun, especially in fraternity and sorority houses, where, according to one study, 86 percent of fraternity residents and 80 percent of sorority residents reported binge drinking (Erenberg and Hacker 1997). College students who binge drink often describe themselves as moderate or light drinkers.[8] Another form of compulsive behavior that is widely accepted in American culture is overeating and an excessive accumulation of material goods. The social acceptance, even encouragement of, excessive shopping can make it difficult to recognize when it is being used compulsively as a way to cope with stress.

When a parishioner initiates a pastoral care conversation about a crisis or life-cycle transition, caregivers have an opportunity to inquire about how they are coping. Family members may seek help from pastoral caregivers when a crisis results from a family member's way of coping with stress. When pastors talk about addictions in their sermons and offer communal prayers for those struggling with recovery, families are more likely to turn to them for help. For example, a teenager using anorexia as a way of coping with the stress of adolescence inevitably involves the family in her restrictive eating. While she will not likely seek help herself, her parents may turn to the youth minister, especially if they know that the youth program includes discussions about compulsive ways of coping like alcohol and drug abuse, anorexia, bingeing, and self-mutilation.

Given how common it is for people to deny compulsive behaviors, pastors need to ask specific questions about overworking, overeating, alcohol, and drug abuse. Detailed questions to ask concerning overworking include: How late do you usually stay at the office? Do you bring work home? Do you typically work in the evening? Do you work on the weekends? Are there times during the week when you deliberately do not work? What are those times like? What is it like when you

---

8. In a national survey Lyall (1995) found that 91 percent of women and 78 percent of men who met the criteria for binge drinking described themselves as moderate or light drinkers.

are on a holiday? Questions about eating patterns include: Is there a particular time in the day when you eat more than you should? What do you usually eat? How much? Do you try to get rid of the food you've eaten by vomiting or using laxatives? Are there times during the day when you think about food and what you will eat? How often does that happen? What happens when you try not to binge or restrict your calories (in the case of anorexia)?

In comparing these sets of questions, it is easy to see how much more difficult it is to ask questions about eating patterns. Overworking is a culturally acceptable way of coping; overeating is not. In asking such questions caregivers must convey an attitude of compassion, not moralistic judgment. Compulsive behaviors are not a result of moral failure; they are attempts to satisfy spiritual hunger and longing. Pastoral caregivers can help careseekers become aware of such hunger.

Compulsive ways of coping can have the immediate effect of making people feel good in superficial and unrealistic ways. The first alcoholic drink or bite of a binge may bring a euphoric sense of well-being. A compulsive gambler buying the first lottery card or making the first bet may be convinced that this time he'll hit the jackpot. People who always use drinking, drugging, or compulsive behavior to cope with stress are not able to tolerate stress long enough to dig deeper psychologically and spiritually and identify its roots. Nelson (2004) uses the powerful metaphor of "the thirst behind the thirst" to describe the existential fears and anxiety that may be the deepest source of stress: the more irresistible the impulse to start a binge, the deeper the existential anxiety fueling the impulse. It was only after he was in recovery from alcohol addiction that Nelson could recognize his need to accept too many writing and speaking engagements as a fear of his own finitude: "Saying 'Yes' to the requests seemed to mean life and actualization, new experiences, relationships, and opportunities. 'No' meant renunciation, relinquishment, passing things up. 'No,' in short, meant finitude—fearful boundaries, restricted space and time, the final limits of death itself" (Nelson 2004, 114).

Compulsive ways of coping can be described as a form of idolatry in which food, alcohol, work, or sex functions as a god in people's lives (Morgan and Jordan 1999; Martignetti 2000). "Why, when it was possible to buy God in a bottle, and drink him off, and become a God oneself, were men not forever drunken?" writes novelist Thomas Wolfe (quoted in Nelson 2004, 27). The idol takes over one's life; the most insidious allegiance to one's idol comes in the form of obsessively thinking about alcohol, work, food, material objects, or sex. The covenant with God is replaced by a covenant with the object of compulsive behavior.

For the person caught in compulsive behaviors, it can seem at moments as if satisfying the compulsion is a way of coping with anxiety so that the covenant with God can be kept. Rationales for compulsive behaviors include

— using Internet pornography releases sexual tension so that I can concentrate without distraction on the rest of my life;
— going shopping and buying clothes makes me feel more self-confident;
— accepting more responsibilities forces me to work more efficiently and stretches me in new directions.

A pastor can counter one of these rationales by gently suggesting that the next time they feel compelled to engage in such behaviors they experiment with a religious or spiritual way of coping with stress, like going for a walk, doing a relaxation exercise that focuses on spiritual or religious imagery, relaxing in a hot bath, sitting in a garden, writing a journal entry, playing a musical instrument, painting, or spending time with a pet. By beginning such activities with prayer, caregivers can use the activity intentionally to connect with a sense of the sacred.

Asking careseekers how they cope with stress can open up the topic of whether and how they use religion or spirituality to cope with stress. Two aspects of religious coping are important to explore: how they relate to God when they experience stress and what kinds of religious activities are used to cope. Pargament and his colleagues (Pargament 1997) have empirically investigated these aspects of religious coping. A consistent finding is that a collaborate style of coping, in which careseekers see themselves as active partners with God,[9] is associated with positive psychological and spiritual outcomes, like stress-related psychological and spiritual growth. The deferring style consists of waiting for and relying upon God.[10] Compared with the collaborative style, the deferring style is "tied to a number of indicators of poorer competence: a lower sense of

9. The following are items from the collaborative religious coping scale: "When it comes to deciding how to solve a problem, God and I work together as partners. When considering a difficult situation, God and I work together to think of possible solutions. After solving a problem, I work with God to make sense of it" (Pargament 1997, 181).

10. The following are sample items on this scale: "Rather than trying to come up with the right solution to a problem myself, I let God decide how to deal with it. I don't spend much time thinking about troubles I've had; God makes sense of them for me" (Pargament 1997, 181).

personal control, lower self-esteem, less planful problem-solving skills, and greater intolerance of differences between people" (Pargament 1997, 182). The deferring style is associated with positive health outcomes, however, when people are in stressful circumstances in which they actually do not have any control over what happens. The third style, self-directing, in which people rely on themselves rather than God,[11] is associated with both positive and negative psychological and spiritual outcome.

In addition to these three styles of religious coping, Pargament and his colleagues have empirically studied which religious coping activities are associated with positive and negative outcome. Seeking spiritual support, reframing a crisis in ways that describe God as benevolent, and getting support from one's community of faith are all associated with positive outcomes. Expressions of discontent with one's community of faith and God, and reframing a crisis in ways that describe God negatively (for example, as punitive) are activities associated with negative outcome. These findings indicate that how careseekers (1) relate to God, in terms of a self-directing, deferring, or collaborative style; (2) relate to their congregations; and (3) frame the crisis in terms of God's benevolence or punishment make a difference and need to be assessed. Simply using one's religion to cope with stress will not ensure positive outcome; what matters is *how* one draws upon religion.

Having considered the role of religion in coping, caregivers can next assess the careseeker's level of motivation. Motivation is a key issue in letting go of compulsive ways of coping. Careseekers who have not yet become psychologically dependent on using compulsive behaviors to cope will be more able to experiment with spiritual ways of coping and report back to the caregiver. If, after three or four conversations, it becomes clear that the careseeker needs more than the supportive care a minister can offer, then referral is necessary. Pastors must have on hand information about weight-management programs like Weight Watchers, and 12-step programs for compulsive behaviors like overeating and compulsive use of pornography. They can also make referrals to pastoral counselors. After making a referral the pastor can continue to support the careseeker in finding meaningful spiritual and religious ways of coping with stress, an aspect of care that might not be addressed in a weight-management program or 12-step group.

Many careseekers will not be sufficiently motivated to change until

---

11. Sample items on the self-directing scale are: "After I've gone through a rough time, I try to make sense of it without relying on God. When faced with trouble, I deal with my feelings without God's help" (Pargament 1997, 181).

they are in crisis—when they hit bottom. For people who compulsively overeat, the crisis will likely be health-related—a heart attack or the onset of borderline diabetes. The workaholic person may discover that his marriage is disintegrating or one of his children is in trouble. The person who compulsively surfs the Internet for pornography may be caught viewing or downloading pornography at home or at work. The person who compulsively shops and accumulates material goods may find herself in deep financial trouble. The person who gambles may accumulate debts. The crisis becomes an opportunity to break the idolatrous covenant with food, work, pornography, material goods, and gambling and return to a covenant with God to satisfy the "thirst behind the thirst." The pastor is in a unique position to reflect spiritually and theologically with careseekers who have hit bottom. With their expertise in assessing spiritual and religious ways of coping and identifying the spiritual roots of compulsive behaviors, they can become part of a caregiving team that includes other healthcare professionals.

Alcoholism and drug addiction differ from other compulsive behaviors in three ways: (1) There is a genetic predisposition that makes people experience the positive effects of the substance more intensely and sometimes lessens negative physical reactions that follow a binge; (2) the addictive substance chemically alters the brain; (3) with tolerance comes a physiological need, experienced in cravings, to consume more of the substance to achieve the same positive effects as before.[12] These factors make alcohol and drug abuse and addiction much more difficult to treat than compulsive behaviors. Pastors do not have the expertise and resources to be the sole caregivers. They can, however, do enough of an assessment to determine that expert help is needed. Often they, unlike other caregivers, will be the first to see signs of addiction.

What are the signs of alcohol addiction?

— The smell of alcohol on someone's breath, especially at times of the day when alcohol is not usually consumed
— Excessive use of alcohol at social events; inebriation at social events
— Unexplained absences from church meetings; difficulty fulfilling responsibilities they have accepted at church
— A pattern of injuries that could be related to inebriation

12. "We alcoholics learned that the ingestion of alcohol produced pleasure in us (how much pleasure seems partly determined by heredity). But the pleasure is short-lived and is followed by feelings of discomfort (the degree to which may also be linked to heredity). . . . The name for the unhappy feeling is *craving* and nothing is as effective in abolishing it as the drug that produced it in the first place" (Nelson 2004, 26).

— Efforts to cut down on drinking
— Signs of withdrawal, like increased hand tremor, sweating, vomiting, physical agitation, evidence of hallucinations

Drug dependence is more difficult to discern; pastors are not likely to see evidence of such dependence.[13]

Someone who abuses or is addicted to alcohol will likely deny or minimize the extent of his or her drinking. The *Harvard Mental Health Letter* notes:

> [D]rinkers are not equally divided into two groups: the healthy and the disordered. Patterns of abusive or immoderate drinking are complicated and vary with the individual; it is not easy to classify either drinking problems or the people who have them, and it is not clear when a problem is serious enough to warrant diagnosis or treatment.
> (*Harvard Mental Health Letter*, May 2000, 1)

Many people who are dependent can maintain long periods of abstinence, which may also make assessment difficult.

The most important component of assessment concerns asking for details about the role that alcohol plays in someone's life. This questioning can begin with general questions about how a careseeker copes with stress, and the caregiver can follow up with detailed questions at that point or later in the conversation. Detailed questions to ask concerning alcohol use include:

> What do you drink? When? How much and how often? How often do you drink more than usual? Do you sometimes feel uncomfortable when alcohol is not available? Are you in more of a hurry to take the first drink than you used to be? . . . Do you sometimes feel guilty about your drinking? Are you annoyed when people talk about your drinking? Are there mornings when you cannot remember parts of the evening before? Do you often regret something you did or said while drinking? Are you constantly making and breaking rules about when, where, and how much to drink?
> (*Harvard Mental Health Letter*, May 2000, 1–2)

These questions about alcohol can be followed with a question about drugs: have you ever used anything else, like marijuana or cocaine?

---

13. Information for parents about detecting drug use by teenagers can be found at the following Web site: http://health.org.

Such questions would be asked as part of a conversation, not in rapid-fire succession. Their variety provides caregivers with different ways to explore alcohol and drug abuse and addiction.

Assessing an individual with compulsive ways of coping is even more complex when the person has other psychological vulnerabilities, like experiences with violence or tendencies toward depression, anxiety, schizophrenia, or bipolar disorder. Pastors are not equipped to diagnosis mental illness. What they can do is encourage persons with addictions to seek treatment first for their addiction, because treatment for mental illness will not be effective until they are in recovery. Drinking and violence often interact with each other. While perpetrators may blame their violence on alcohol or drugs, in fact, they use these substances to excess knowing that they will in turn become violent.

Substance abuse and addiction have dramatic effects on relational systems. A household that includes an alcoholic person inevitably becomes an alcoholic family, with alcohol an unnamed member of the family that functions in an overpowering way. The family system gradually shifts in order to accommodate the addiction and abuse. Children learn to take over when a parent is drunk. A wife tells her husband's boss that he is ill when he has a hangover. Teenagers are permitted to sleep off a binge undisturbed. Members of the extended family may provide loans when the family provider is unemployed because of alcohol abuse or addiction. Having access to the family in ways that mental health professionals don't, pastors can identify the role of addiction in a family and break the silence. They can make referrals for assessment and treatment and provide family members with information about 12-step groups.

The goal of assessment is to gather enough preliminary information to determine whether medical assessment and care is warranted. Pastors do not have the expertise to be primary caregivers; however, they can make referrals and be a supportive presence in the life of someone who abuses or is addicted to alcohol or other substances. According to Dann (2002) this supportive presence needs to include patience, honesty, withholding judgment, and maintaining personal boundaries. Patience is necessary because persons with addictions will often not begin recovery until they have hit bottom. Establishing honesty is important because addicts use dishonesty to maintain their habits and conceal its effects. "Something as seemingly simple as honesty strikes at the heart of an addict's denial, hiding, and scheming, without which his or her dysfunction cannot continue" (Dann 2002, 46). Withholding judgment is part of understanding addictions as a disease, not as a moral failing. Maintaining personal boundaries becomes necessary when caregivers feel compelled to rescue someone who has gotten into trouble because of an addiction. Protecting a person with an addiction from the consequences of his or her actions will only prolong her or his addiction. "Suffering consequences is the primary way that an addict concludes that he or she needs to quit or get help" (Dann 2002, 49). Caregivers need to set limits on their availability if a person in recovery requires round-the-clock support. A sponsor from Alcoholics Anonymous or Narcotics Anonymous can provide such support. Pastoral caregivers must use a team approach, working closely with addiction counselors and organizations like Alcoholics Anonymous, approaches that emphasize powerlessness, the need for group support and the support of a sponsor, especially during the early days of recovery.

EXERCISE 5: ASSESSING LOSS, VIOLENCE, AND COPING

Readers may use the following guidelines to assess the extent to which loss, violence, and compulsive ways of coping are part of the careseeker's crisis.

1. Assess whether loss is part of the problem:
   a. Address the following questions:

   — Is the careseeker in the acute or long-term phase of grief?
   — Is he or she (1) experiencing a range of intense reactions like anger, disbelief, guilt, and sadness; and (2) having trouble eating and sleeping?
   — Is he or she in the long-term phase of reconstructing their lives?

   b. Describe the losses that may feature in a careseeker's crisis. Consider whether this crisis is part of a single transition or concurrent life-cycle transitions. For example, a person who has recently divorced his spouse and married a second spouse who has children is going through three life-cycle transitions: divorce, becoming married again, and establishing a stepfamily. Using the chart below, identify the losses in terms of the six categories. For example, when a divorced person loses his or her home, note "loss of home" beside material loss. When a person breaks her leg, note "temporary loss of mobility" under functional loss.

Category of Loss	One column for each concurrent life-cycle transition		
Material Loss			
Relational Loss			
Intrapsychic Loss			
Functional Loss			
Role Loss			
Systemic Loss			

2. Assess whether violence is part of the problem by addressing the following questions:

— Is violence a part of the careseeker's crisis and/or story? What type(s) of violence have occurred: physical violence, psychological violence, sexual violence, neglect? Look beyond the immediate crisis to consider the careseeker's family of origin, extended family, community, and cultural systems, and take stock of any and all types of violence in all of these relationships.

— To what extent is the careseeker experiencing posttraumatic stress by alternating between reexperiencing traumatic events and being emotionally disengaged and numb? How much do these responses to violence disrupt or interfere with the careseeker's life? How long has the careseeker been experiencing posttraumatic stress or disorder?

3. Assess the careseeker's coping ability:

a. Name the careseeker's ways of coping by referencing how she or he attempts to deal with suffering. Note the presence of any of the following symptoms:

— Avoiding emotions having to do with grief, and keeping feelings bottled up

— Expressing only the anger associated with grieving a loss arising out of violence

— Using addictive substances (nicotine, alcohol, drugs)

— Using compulsive behaviors (overeating, overworking, anorexia, gambling, compulsive shopping, use of pornography) to numb feelings and endure the passage of time

— Being self-reliant and not trusting anyone else with the processing of grief, particularly in terms of not taking opportunities that come along to connect with those who reach out

b. Note the extent to which such coping helps the careseeker do the following:

— Deal with the immediate distress of acute loss and stress
— Endure the intensity of grief and stress responses
— Connect them more deeply with themselves, God, and with those whom they have empathic and empowering relationships
— Disengage them from such meaningful relationships
— Foster a sense of self-agency that allows them to act in empowering ways, OR foster a brief sense of self-agency (as, for example, may be the case with compulsive exercising and shopping) that may allow for a superficial, and often sentimental expression of feelings

c. To what extent do they use their religious/spiritual traditions to cope with stress? Psychologically evaluate their use of religion and spirituality (chapter 7 on theological reflection describes ways of theologically assessing such coping) by answering the series of questions in b. Besides looking at the careseeker's explicit references to her or his religious/spiritual identity, consider settings where religious symbols are available to them, such as in funeral services, in graveyards, in a community of faith, and in the culture around them, such as shrines and memorials that mark places or commemorate tragedy. Do such symbols and practices seem to offer ways of coping that are used by the careseeker?

4. Assess the risk of suicide by considering this question: Does the careseeker seem so overwhelmed by the crisis that he or she might consider suicide?

6

Systemic Assessment: The Careseeker's Culture, Communities, and Family

In chapter 5, we examined understanding a careseeker's story in terms of loss, violence, and compulsive ways of coping. I now describe the next step of pastoral care: assessing the careseeker's closest relationships, current family, family of origin, communities, and culture. In what ways do these relational systems help the careseeker mourn her losses, survive violence, and cope with stress? Do any of them intensify her suffering?

Systemic assessment is necessary for three reasons. First, a careseeker does not exist in isolation; her life is inextricably interwoven with the lives of a partner and/or close friends, her family, and those with whom she lives, works, and worships. Her psychological, physical, and spiritual health is nurtured or threatened by relational systems of family, friends, church, and culture. Second, the narratives she constructs to make sense of her life are shaped by the stories told in her family, church, and in the culture. Some of these stories have the power to transform her life; others limit the ways in which she makes sense of what has happened. Third, caring for persons goes hand in hand with caring for families and communities. In order for transformation to take place in a person's life, it will also need to happen in his relational systems: his relationship with his partner, friends, family, and co-workers.

I begin with a case study and then discuss the role of the cultural system in a careseeker's crisis in general and in reference to the case study.

I move on to the role of community and then discuss relationships with one's partner and friends and the careseeker's historical and present family. While all of the systems I've described (psychological, spiritual, familial, and cultural) shape each other, it is helpful to assess each system separately, especially in terms of planning care that addresses the vulnerabilities and uses the strengths of each systemic level.

Case Study

Patsy Rodrigues is a student chaplain at St. Mary's Hospital in Sante Fe, New Mexico. She has been asked to visit a Roman Catholic patient, twenty-year-old Maria Sanchez, in the maternity ward. Maria gave birth by Caesarean section to a premature baby who died two hours later. She is a recent immigrant from Mexico. Although Patsy is not Roman Catholic, she has been asked to see Maria because she speaks Spanish fluently. Their conversation takes place in a ward with four patients. The curtain is pulled around Maria's bed. When Patsy opens the curtain she sees that Maria is staring out the window. Her eyes are red from recent tears.

Patsy (1): Hello, Ms. Sanchez, I'm Patsy, one of the chaplains here. I'm so sorry to hear about the death of your baby.

Maria (1): He was so beautiful; so tiny, and so beautiful. They took him away so quickly. They said he was sick. If only I could have just held him.

Patsy (2): It must be such a shock that they couldn't save his life.

Maria (2): They said he couldn't breathe. He was struggling so hard to get his breath. I felt so helpless. (She begins to cry.)

Patsy (3): I'm so sorry. (They sit in silence.)

Maria (3): I was working too hard and then my water broke and the labor pains started.

Patsy (4): What do you mean—you were working too hard?

Maria (4): I clean houses. But you won't tell anyone, will you? (She looks suddenly afraid.) I'm not supposed to work.

Patsy (5): No, I won't tell anyone.

Maria (5): I clean houses with a group of women. That's how I've been able to live since I came here.

Patsy (6): It sounds like you're worried that labor started because of the physical work you were doing.

Maria (6): Yes. My back had started to hurt a few days ago. I think it was a warning. But I kept working.

Patsy (7): You weren't able to see a doctor?

Maria (7): I couldn't pay. I don't know how I will pay for this hospital. The women in the apartment where I live brought me to the emergency room when the baby started to come.

Patsy (8): Let me talk with someone in the hospital who may be able to help out. (Silence.) You must have been very frightened when the baby was coming. And then they had to deliver the baby by doing a Caesarean section.

Maria (8): The pain was so bad. My friend stayed with me and helped me understand that I couldn't deliver the baby; they had to operate.

Patsy (9): That must have been so hard. It's good your friend was there. (There is a pause in the conversation.) I wonder if you would like to come with me and see your baby. The nurse wanted me to tell you that you could. They have him in a quiet room where we can sit together.

Maria (9): (Crying) Yes, could I? (Patsy leaves to get a nursing assistant to help Maria into a wheelchair. Patsy takes her to a quiet, darkened room, where the body of Maria's baby is in a bassinet, wrapped tightly in a blanket. She lifts the baby up and places him in Maria's arms. Mary rocks back and forth, weeping.)

Maria (10): O dear God, he is so beautiful. Why did he die?

Patsy (10): Yes, he is beautiful. He is one of God's beloved children.

Maria (11): O, my poor baby! I wanted to call him Juan after my brother.

Patsy (11): Juan, what a lovely name.

Maria (12): Do you think I can look at him, at his body, I mean?

Patsy (12): Yes, of course. You hold him and I'll unwrap the blanket.

Maria (13): Look at his feet! So tiny! And his little hands. (Maria bends down and kisses his fingers.)

Patsy (13): Yes.

Maria (14): Can you baptize him? I want him to be in heaven.

Patsy (14): I believe he's with God right now. I'm not sure if I can baptize him. But for now I can say a prayer of blessing. Would that be okay?

Maria (15): Yes.

Patsy (15): Here. Put your hand on his head. (Patsy places her hand on top of Maria's.) Dear God, we thank you for Juan, for his life. You knit him together in his mother's womb, forming his bones, knowing every moment of his life. He is your beloved son, and we know you love him so much. It is so hard for us to let go of his body—to no longer be able to care for his body and help him grow. We know that his soul is with you now, embraced by your love. Please look after him and take care of him, the way his mother would. You are his mother now, and his father. We entrust him to you. Amen.

Maria (16): Amen. (Crying.) Yes, God is taking care of him now. (They sit together in silence for ten minutes. Then Maria gives a deep sigh. She wraps the blanket around the baby.)

Maria (17): He is gone now. He is with God.

Patsy (17): Yes.

Maria (18): Can I bury his body?

Patsy (18): I don't know. Shall I see if one of the nurses can come in, and you can ask her? (Patsy asks the nursing supervisor to join them, and they talk with Maria about how she can make arrangements for a funeral.)

Assessing a Careseeker's Culture and Social Identity

To assess the effects of cultural systems on a careseeker's crisis, caregivers examine how the careseeker's narrative and identity are shaped by her culture, that is, the practices that transmit a culture's knowledge, beliefs, morals, law, and customs. Caregivers are especially interested in the careseeker's access to social resources, and the ways in which the careseeker's status within culture gives or denies power in all its forms: financial, professional, organizational, or educational (Gergen 2001). In the case study, Patsy considers how Maria's crisis is shaped by her Mexican, Roman Catholic culture. Patsy intuits that Maria's desire to have the body of her baby baptized reflects her Roman Catholic belief that, without baptism, her baby's soul will not go to heaven. Patsy is not sure whether a priest, doing this pastoral visit, would baptize the body. She needs to ask the Roman Catholic chaplain this question, and then have another conversation about baptism with Maria.

Patsy also reflects on how Maria's social status as an immigrant without a work permit and health insurance exacerbates her crisis. She will have a staggering bill to pay. Disclosing information about her financial status to the hospital's billing department could help her qualify for aid, but she may be fearful about giving them any further information about herself. Her anxiety will be heightened by her difficulties understanding English. Patsy can reflect further on the role of culture in Maria's crisis by thinking about her social identity.

"Social identity" is the identity one is given in a social context when a feature of one's self like gender is classified in socially determined categories like male/female/transgender.[1] This identity is socially assigned and can bring with it social advantages and disadvantages. Being identified, for example, as a young person may be advantageous in one social context and detrimental in another. A minister who appears young for her age may be more readily accepted by members of her youth group and questioned for her seeming lack of experience by older congregational members. In this example, there may be an interaction between several features of Patsy—her gender, youthful appearance, petite size, her soft-spoken manner of speech—that prompt older members to judge her as too inexperienced.

A kaleidoscope is a good metaphor for describing how features of one's self interact in the formation of social identity. Each piece of colored glass represents a feature of one's social identity; together the pieces form a pattern. When the kaleidoscope is turned (like the construction

---

1. Identity has been traditionally described in Euro-American cultures as "a sense of personal coherence through time and changing role requirements, a sense of one's value and consistent contributions to one's social world" (Okun et al. 1999, 137–38, referring to the work of Erik Erikson). A distinction can be made between the "self-as-subject (the one who knows) and self-as-object (the one who is known or observed)" (Okun et al. 1999). From a psychosocial perspective, identity is shaped by the various dynamic systems of which we are a part, that is, by subjective psychological systems and family, communal, and cultural systems. The shaping of identity is a dialogical process (Taylor 1992) that uses language and various modes of relating with others. As Taylor says, "We define our identity always in dialogue with, sometimes in struggle against, the things our significant others want to see in us" (Taylor 1992, reprinted in Goldberg 1994, 79).

of another social identity in a different context), the fragments of glass are rearranged and form a new pattern. Similarly, in one's cultural context, the different features of social identity do not disappear but are reconfigured as one moves from context to context.

An important part of understanding a careseeker's social identity involves determining whether aspects of her identity are positively regarded and give her access to material, psychological, and social resources. Being identified as well educated because of one's appearance and manner of speech will be an advantage in many social contexts. In the case study, if Maria were a Euro-American woman without financial resources because she was in graduate school, she might be treated differently by members of the hospital staff. She would more likely have access to resources from her family and be better equipped to seek aid.

It is often difficult for a caregiver who experiences social privilege to identify the role played by either social identity or oppression in a careseeker's story. Caregivers who have access to financial, professional, emotional, and social support because of their own social identity may not recognize these social privileges and may unconsciously assume that everyone has similar access. Without critical reflection upon lifelong social privilege, white middle-class caregivers will not recognize their inevitable participation in systemic racism (Ramsay 2002). In the case study, Patsy may feel overwhelmed by Maria's need for help with settling her hospital bill, finding a priest, and arranging a funeral; she may find herself wishing that Maria would just disappear—leave the hospital, leave New Mexico, and "go back to where she came from."

Caregivers can assess a careseeker's social identity by considering features of her identity separately—first gender, then race, then social class, and so on—and determining whether each feature is likely to be socially advantageous or disadvantageous in her current crisis. In considering a careseeker's gender, for example, the caregiver can reflect on whether the careseeker is at an advantage or disadvantage because of his or her gender. In order to appreciate the complexity of social identity, caregivers must consider all possible features that could be salient in the careseeker's crisis—like being married/single/divorced, being physically attractive or unattractive, being slender/overweight/obese, and so on.

A Euro-American middle-class man who is elderly and frail may, for example, experience gender as a disadvantage at this phase of life. If he has experienced a sense of control because of the social privileges that came with being white, male, and middle class, then he may find the loss of control that comes with aging particularly difficult to experience.

He may feel overwhelmed by his anger, an emotion which in the past has helped him take charge, but which now masks feelings like sadness and despair, which he is not able to recognize and express. In his example, gender, age, and social class interact to create social disadvantages. Contrast the example of this man with that of an African American woman, always poor, now frail and elderly. Her social identity may have caused her to suffer, which in turn may have deepened her religious faith and connections with her faith community. Her ability to cope with suffering may be a resource that provides a sense of spiritual well-being.

Ultimately the purpose of assessing a careseeker's social identity is threefold. The caregiver (1) gains an understanding of the careseeker's experience of social oppression, (2) anticipates the kind of help the careseeker will need when the caregiver develops a plan of care (see chapter 8), and (3) identifies the social systems that will have to be transformed before full healing and justice are possible. In the case study, reflecting on Maria's social identity deepens Patsy's understanding of Maria's social oppression as a young woman, an immigrant without a work permit or health insurance, and as a non-English-speaker. She can anticipate that Maria will need different kinds of help: spiritual, psychological, medical, financial, and legal. Ultimately, Maria's well-being depends upon whether she will be cared for by a society in which medical care is available to everyone and in which she can earn a living without fear of legal reprisals.

Assessing Local Community/Organizational Systems

Careseekers may be part of a variety of community or organizational systems: a religious community of faith, an educational system, the place where they work, professional organizations, and recreational groups. These systems and organizations can offer support to a careseeker or might make life more difficult. Caregivers can assess the role of these community systems and organizations by asking: Does being part of this community system or organization support or undermine a careseeker as she mourns losses during the acute or long-term phase of grief, seeks safety and recovery from violence, or lets go of compulsive behaviors and finds healthy ways to cope?

Caregivers must first identify any destructive or malevolent effects of communities or organizations. The ignorance, prejudice, and gossip of people within a community system or organization can greatly exacerbate the careseeker's suffering. After identifying the problem, the minister and careseeker can plan what action to take. It may be possible to educate and/or confront the offending parties. When the caregiver is the minister of a community of faith that responds in this way, she or he can speak prophetically and challenge members to love their neighbors as themselves. Clergy can also take action in their local community; for example, they can work with school administrators when a student is being bullied or harassed, and in circumstances where there is a risk of hate crimes because of the careseeker's racial or sexual identity, caregivers must assess such risks and include plans for safety.

If it is not possible to change or leave the community or organization that is exacerbating the careseeker's suffering, then caregiver and careseeker can try to protect the careseeker psychologically and spiritually in whatever ways are possible. If, for example, the workplace is the problem, the careseeker can try various strategies. She can do deep breathing and use muscle relaxation techniques that help her gain psychological distance from others at work. She can take breaks that get her out of her work environment. She can place pictures or objects in her work environment that help her connect with a sense of life as sacred. On the way home from work she can use prayer and relaxation exercises to cope with the accumulated stress of the day.

After addressing problematic dynamics in the community systems or organizations of which the careseeker is a member, the caregiver can consider whether becoming a member of a healthy group could enhance the careseeker's healing. A community of faith or specific support group can offer nonjudgmental and compassionate care. Such support can be likened to the plain simple goodness of bread for the hungry.

How would Patsy Rodrigues, the student chaplain in the case study, assess the role of community or organizational systems in Maria's crisis? Reflecting on their conversation, Patsy recalls that it was one of the women with whom Maria works and lives who brought her to the hospital. Patsy wonders how much emotional support and help Maria receives from them. She is aware that they will not likely be able to help Maria with her financial problems; however, they may know about community resources if they have survived for long in this country. Patsy also wonders whether Maria is part of a community of faith, what her community is like, and if not, if there is a Roman Catholic parish that could provide her with support and help. These are questions she can pursue when she helps Maria make arrangements for the burial.

Assessing Family of Origin and/or Present Family

Caregivers can assess whether the careseeker's family is a help or a hindrance by looking at the power dynamics and relational boundaries in the family system (Doehring 1995). In the midst of the careseeker's crisis, are family members able to relate to each other in ways that are empathic? Can they stay in touch with each other's humanity, honoring the mystery and complexity of each family member? Or do they become disengaged from each other's humanity, and fused with distorted images of each other? In terms of power dynamics, can they negotiate a healthy balance of give and take, knowing when to recognize and acknowledge the other's need and when to assert one's own needs? Or do they become caught in power struggles, wanting to overpower and feeling overpowered? How are these power struggles resolved? These are the kinds of questions that caregivers can ask in assessing the family system.

Caregivers can further assess family systems by considering how family dynamics may reflect cultural and religious traditions concerning sex roles (the roles of husband/wife, father/mother, for example). Graham (1992) has used family systems theory in conjunction with cultural systems theory to address power imbalances that are culturally contextual, that is, power imbalances experienced within a family because of age, gender, sexual orientation, or physical or mental appearance and/or ability. He uses the term "demonic hegemony" to describe the potential for evil that exists in intractable power imbalances in the culture that are acted upon in the family. A nuclear family, for example, may reflect an ethnic heritage rooted in northern Europe by becoming emotionally disengaged from each other in the midst of a crisis. Those who are vulnerable and dependent in the family system are psychologically abandoned. There is no help from outside because the family has isolated itself from the community, keeping its problems private and self-contained.

In seeking to understand the relation between the family and cultural systems, caregivers can sometimes draw upon cultural stereotypes that do not do justice to the complexity of cultures and families, especially when the caregiver is identified with a race or ethnicity that is socially advantaged and the careseeker is identified with one that is not. In the case study, while Patsy and Maria are both Hispanic, Patsy's world is quite different from Maria's. Patsy needs to be careful that she doesn't form judgments of Maria's family or the father of Maria's child.

If she has the opportunity for further pastoral care conversations in which she can hear the story of Maria's family in all of its complexity, then she will be better able to assess the connections between Maria's family system and her culture.

Another dimension of family assessment concerns the family system that the careseeker experienced when growing up. People in crisis often reexperience the family dynamics that occurred during childhood crises and transitions. They may, for example, reexperience the helplessness and vulnerability they felt as a child or adolescent, and how they and their family members coped. If a person's parents were compassionate and supportive, memories of being safe and able to trust others will be resources. If one's parents were helpless or reacted in abusive or neglectful ways, those memories may cause a great sense of danger or fear. In many ways the family of origin experience becomes an internalized relational map that can be a primary way of making sense of what is happening in the middle of a crisis. If a person has not had experiences in which these formative relational dynamics were transformed, there is a danger that the early family dynamics will be reenacted in the current crisis. This occurs, for example, when substance abuse and family violence recur in some of the children in the next generation.

While pastoral caregivers do not have the psychological expertise to see how careseekers may be enacting relational dynamics from their family of origin, they can be alert to signs that the careseeker is psychologically "stuck." A careseeker whose grief seems disproportionate to the losses he has recently experienced may be facing unmourned losses from childhood. A parishioner who becomes intensely emotionally attached to her minister may be reexperiencing complex dynamics in her relationship with her father. Pastors with a healthy awareness of their own boundaries will be able to sense when a psychological drama from a careseeker's family of origin is being reenacted in the pastoral relationship. These signs indicate that the careseeker needs to be referred for counseling.

There are pastoral occasions when it is appropriate for the minister to gather extensive information about the careseeker's family of origin for psychoeducational purposes. These occasions occur when careseekers are not in crisis and are seeking help navigating a life-cycle transition like becoming married and having children. A psychoeducational tool that has been used widely to help people understand themselves in relation to their families of origin is the genogram, which is a diagram of the family tree. The minister can demonstrate how to draw the family tree, using the following standard set of symbols. A square is used for men and boys and a circle for girls and women. The birth date can be written above the circle or square. If the person is deceased, an "x" is made in the circle or square and the year of death may be noted. The age is written within the circle or square. Marriage is indicated by drawing a connecting solid line between two people:

m. 1970

A relationship in which people are living together or having an affair is noted with a dotted line in place of the solid line. Separation is indicated with a slash in the line, divorce with two slashes. Children are ranked in birth order beginning with the oldest on the left:

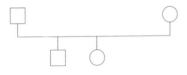

For a more detailed description of how to construct a genogram, caregivers can consult Anderson and Fite (1994) and McGoldrick, Gerson, and Shellenberger (1999).

Careseekers can be taught the basics of how to construct their genogram and complete it between meetings with the minister. In premarital counseling, the genogram can be used as a way for a couple to understand each other's family dynamics. They can reflect on whether they see patterns in how they each handle relational conflict compared with their parents. The genogram can also be used in meeting with parents for baptismal counseling, to reflect with them on patterns in how they were raised and how they are raising their children. As a psychoeducational tool, the genogram can prompt careseekers to reflect upon family dynamics as they move through life-cycle transitions like becoming married and becoming parents.

Assessing Intimate Partnerships and Friendships

Caregivers can make a basic assessment of whether the careseeker is in a healthy intimate relationship by asking whether within the marriage spouses or partners have respect for each other. Gottman describes a healthy marriage:

> Happily married couples . . . in their day-to-day lives . . . have hit upon a dynamic that keeps their negative thoughts and feelings about each other (which all couples have) from overwhelming their positive ones. They have what I call an emotionally intelligent marriage.
>
> (Gottman 1999, 3)

In contrast, "In an unhappy marriage people experience chronic, diffuse physiological arousal—in other words, they feel physically stressed and usually emotionally stressed as well" (Gottman 1999, 5). Happily married couples "share a deep sense of meaning. They don't just 'get along.' They also support each other's hopes and aspirations and build a sense of purpose into their lives together. This is really what I mean when I talk about honoring and respecting each other" (Gottman 1999, 23).

Besides asking about whether there is a basic quality of respect in a careseeker's marriage, the caregiver can ask questions similar to the ones used to assess the health of a family system. Is their spouse or partner able to listen compassionately when the careseeker expresses intense feelings? Is a wife able to stay connected with her husband (the careseeker) in ways that are supportive, while not becoming overly identified with him, such that she can't see where his pain ends and hers begins? Or does the husband of a careseeker tend to be emotionally disengaged when she is in distress? In terms of power dynamics, when there are conflicting needs, can they negotiate a healthy give-and-take, knowing when to recognize and acknowledge the other's need and when to assert one's own needs? Or do they become caught in power struggles, wanting to overpower and feeling overpowered? How are these power struggles resolved?

Pastoral caregivers are not equipped to provide long-term marital therapy. They can make an assessment of whether the marital relationship is a major impediment to the careseeker's healing, provide crisis intervention on a short-term basis, and recommend marital therapy. The crisis experienced by the careseeker may spark a marital crisis in a relationship that was already fragile; the crisis may also create an opportunity for the marriage to be strengthened.

EXERCISE 6: ASSESSING CULTURE, COMMUNITY/ ORGANIZATIONAL, FAMILY, AND MARRIAGE

1. Assessing Social Identity

List all of the aspects of the careseeker's social identity that may be salient in terms of affording the careseeker (1) social advantages that may ameliorate her/his crisis because of access to social resources, or (2) disadvantages that may make this crisis more difficult because of lack of access to social resources. Write a paragraph about each (you may decide to limit your discussion to the five most significant aspects of identity). You may choose to pair interacting aspects of identity and talk about them together. Consider, for example, my description of the social identity of the young female minister: "there may be an interaction between several features of herself—her gender, youthful appearance, petite size, her soft-spoken manner of speech—that prompt older members to judge her as too inexperienced" (p. 101); also see my description of the elderly and frail Euro-American middle-class man (pp. 102–3).

2. Assessing Community and Organizational Systems

Identify and describe any community or organizational systems that are a resource to the careseeker, or are intensifying his or her suffering.

3. Assessing Family and Marital Systems

If you have sufficient information about the careseeker's family and marriage, describe the current family system, the family of origin, and the marital system, using the following questions:

— In the midst of the careseeker's crisis, are family members/the spouse able to relate to each other in ways that are empathic? Can they stay in touch with each other's humanity, honoring the mystery and complexity of each family member? If you have information about the careseeker's family of origin, you can use these questions to consider what happened in the family of origin when there was a crisis.

— Do family members/spouses become disengaged from each other's humanity and fused with distorted images of each other?

— In terms of power dynamics, can they negotiate a healthy give-and-take, knowing when to recognize and acknowledge the other's need and when to assert one's own needs?

— Do they become caught in power struggles, wanting to overpower and feeling overpowered? How are these power struggles resolved?

At the end of each paragraph, make a final assessment of whether the careseeker needs to be referred for (1) family/marital counseling if the family/marital system seems to be so dysfunctional that it is a major impediment in the careseeker's well-being, and/or (2) counseling if the careseeker's suffering seems to arise from family-of-origin dynamics.

7

Theological Reflection

People become most aware of their values when they reach turning points in their lives and must make choices or when they are thrust into decision making because of a crisis. Prior to such moments, they may not have thought much about the values that orient them to the meaning and purpose of their lives. At its simplest, theology is a way to talk about people's deepest values.

The use of theology is what makes pastoral care distinct from other forms of care.[1] Pastoral caregivers can cast in high relief questions about religious faith and meanings, questions that are often ignored or undervalued by those using medical and psychological perspectives. Pastoral caregivers can assess theologically how people put into practice the values that form their religious orientation by asking questions like these: Do their religious faith and practices give people new life, or exacerbate already painful circumstances? To what extent do people ex fullness and complexity of God's presence with them?

Take, for example, the case of Mrs. Reynolds, who has ad cer and prays for a miraculous recovery. George Winston, palian minister, will evaluate whether Mrs. Reynolds's pray that she understands the gravity of her illness or that she is u unable to face the harsh losses that are part of her conditio

---

1. Some have described pastoral caregivers as clinical theologians (Morgan and Jordan 1999) and theologians of care (Schlauch 1995).

want God to cure her cancer and take away her suffering. Do her prayers become so egocentric at moments of denial that there is no room for the mystery of a God who does not simply comply with her heartfelt wishes? Do her prayers for a miraculous recovery hold in tension her denial and acceptance of her cancer? The pastoral caregiver's task is to help sort out the theologically life-giving uses of prayer from the life-denying or destructive uses of prayer. George Winston's initial task in undertaking such assessment is identifying Mrs. Reynolds's embedded theology.

Embedded vs. Deliberative Theology

Everyone who has grappled with deep losses and experiences that threaten their physical and emotional well-being has faced the challenge of making sense of such suffering. People in crisis initially raise questions and make laments, like "why is this happening to me?" Their first attempts at answers come out of their embedded theology, out of the theological presuppositions that shape their lives and practices. Embedded theology is "what devoted Christians have in mind when they say things like 'My faith and my church mean a lot to me'" (Stone and Duke 1996, 15). Embedded theologies are often put into words at funerals when visitors offer comfort to the bereaved. "She's in heaven with God's angels," someone might say, standing before the closed coffin. When a death is sudden and tragic, a friend might say, "I guess God needed her in heaven." "Wrapped up in such a simple statement is a host of associated elements—memories, beliefs, feelings, values, and hopes—not necessarily stated, and perhaps not at all clear" (Stone and Duke 1996, 15). In contrast, deliberative theologies are deliberately thought out; the "host of associated elements" is sorted out—the memories unpacked, the beliefs appraised, the feelings, values, and hopes identified and evaluated.

When people become aware of their embedded theology in the midst of a crisis, they often go through a process of evaluating their beliefs and constructing new ones. As they do this, they are engaging in deliberative theology, "the understanding of faith that emerges from a process of carefully reflecting upon embedded theological convictions" (Stone and Duke 1996, 16). While embedded theologies are accrued over time, sometimes outside of people's conscious awareness, deliberative theologies, in contrast, are actively constructed.

The more public a crisis is, the more likely it is that people will be called to account for their beliefs and as a result engage in deliberative theology. When President Clinton was called to account for his sexual relationship with Monica Lewinsky, and he made public his private rationalization of his behavior, it was clear that he was not living out the promises he had made in marriage or in assuming the office of president. As a result of this public accounting and his acknowledgment of his transgressions, he began a long process of deliberative theology with his spiritual advisors, a process in which he might never have engaged if his behavior had remained a secret. A less dramatic example of the way a public crisis forces people to engage in deliberative theology is a parishioner who has struggled privately with not being able to fulfill her responsibilities at work, and who must come to terms with whether or not she can do her job when her supervisor puts her on probation. When she talks about her struggles with her minister, she has an opportunity to reflect theologically on how painful it has been never to measure up at work, what her real gifts and talents are, and what her vocation is.

As a pastoral caregiver listens to a careseeker articulate the values by which she is trying to live her life, he can take note of whether her embedded theology is congruent with her worldview but at odds with the theology of her religious tradition. In living out her embedded theology, the careseeker may be responding to a revelation of God that is not part of her religious tradition. For example, a Roman Catholic couple uses contraceptives because they are not ready to have a child. In articulating their reasons for not following their tradition's theology on procreation, they may put into words new ways of making theological sense of birth control decisions. They may, for example, describe a sense of God with them in the choices they must make about becoming parents—a sense of God that is dramatically different from the God described by religious church leaders. Their deliberative theology will lead them to reconstruct the Vatican's theology on birth control. Other Roman Catholics might deliberate on the practice of using birth control and decide that the theology underlying the injunction against birth control is true for them in their context. Their deliberative theology will lead them to affirm the Vatican's theology concerning birth control.

When pastor and careseeker engage in deliberative theology, they are seeking God in the midst of the careseeker's experiences of loss and violence, and in his or her struggles to cope with life. They may find the

God he or she has known all along: the immanent presence, like the oxygen in the air that sustains life. Or the careseeker may see God in wholly new ways, as though scales have fallen from his or her eyes; it will be as if the transcendent God, full of mystery, is glimpsed, as Job saw God in the whirlwind. When a minister and careseeker begin to deliberate theologically about who God is now, in this moment, they embark on a journey. They may find themselves pulled in two directions: conserving traditional theologies and reconstructing them.[2]

These two basic theological perspectives lead to polarization in the face of controversial theological issues. Gender, for example, has been a controversial issue for Christian religious traditions in the past fifty years. Those in a reconstructing mode challenge the patriarchal aspects of religious traditions, especially in terms of women's roles in the family and the ordained ministry of the church. The move from male-dominated to gender-inclusive images of God also involves a radical change from centuries-old doctrines and practices in which God was singularly identified as male.

Generally speaking, a conserving orientation is part of premodern and modern approaches to knowledge in which theological propositions are true in all times and places. A postmodern approach to knowledge assumes that knowledge about God must be continually reconstructed in order to be relevant in complex historical contexts. The term "culture wars" has been used to describe religious debates that pit those using premodern and modern approaches against those who use postmodern approaches.

This distinction between postmodern reconstructing theological approaches and premodern and modern conserving theological approaches can be seen in the use of deliberative theology in pastoral care. Take, for example, caring for a transgender person in anguish because his male biology is at odds with his conviction that God intended him to be female. How might one proceed? One minister may search sacred texts for references that can be used as absolute theological propositions for transgender persons in all times and places. Another minister may reflect upon this transgender person's suffering in terms of the rigid social categories used to classify people as either male or female, the mystery of how God creates us in our mother's womb and knows us through and through, and how God is present with those suffering in this particular way. The first minister uses delib-

---

2. Pargament (1997) uses similar terms to describe how religion can be used to cope with stress in ways that either conserve or transform the sacred (or that which is significant).

erative theology to find absolute truth claims based on biblical texts. The second uses deliberative theology to explore the social context of the problem, and construct provisional ways to understand how God is present in this social context, and especially with those who suffer.

A second example involves premarital counseling with cohabitating couples. Pastoral caregivers using a reconstructing theology will explore this couple's experience especially in terms of how conflict is handled, whether they hold each other in mutual regard, and the faith claims upon which they base their commitment. Together, the minister and the couple will deliberate over what God wants for them as a couple. The faith claims that emerge from this deliberative theology will become the basis for decisions about the future of the relationship, especially in terms of becoming married. In contrast, pastoral caregivers using premodern and modern deliberative theologies are likely to apply prescribed norms of behavior. These norms usually take one of two forms: either pastors require that couples live separately before marriage; or pastors simply ignore a couple's experience of cohabitation and get on with their standard premarital sessions.

Pastoral caregivers must incorporate a hermeneutics of suspicion into the process of engaging with careseekers in deliberative theology. Those in a reconstructive mode need to be suspicious of their use of contemporary sources and norms of authority that may not be relevant in a particular context. A caregiver may be so wedded to a particular psychological and theological perspective that she brings it to bear upon every pastoral care encounter without using a hermeneutic of suspicion that prompts her to reflect further on the particular person seeking care. Similarly, in a global context, pastoral theologians writing about pastoral care in North America often assume that their psychological perspectives on pastoral careseekers will be relevant in African or Asian contexts. They need to reflect critically on the basic psychological assumptions that inform their understanding of pastoral care and recognize them as local, not universal assumptions.

What hermeneutics of suspicion are needed with pastoral caregivers and careseekers whose theological deliberations lead them to conserve a traditional doctrine, for instance, a belief that homosexual practices are sinful? They need to pay attention to any group of people who are marginalized by religious traditions, such as women in patriarchal religious traditions, sexual minority persons in heterosexist traditions, and the disabled in traditions that assume able-bodiedness for everyone and attribute disabilities and illness to individual sinfulness. Many religious traditions have been seen in retrospect to oppress those on their margins, and pastoral caregivers should be ready to stand with those who have less power in the tradition, in order to determine whether their experience of the system is benevolent or oppressive.

As pastoral caregivers listen for the embedded theologies that are put into words by people in crisis, in the form of existential questions and laments, they can be attuned to a careseeker's need at times for theological certainty. In the initial shock and denial of acute moments of crisis, people often function out of a premodern mode, appealing directly to God to intervene in their crisis. As they initially express their embedded theologies, they may state absolute convictions about God, which do not take into account rational or scientific understandings. Pastoral caregivers can, in such situations, do their own deliberative theological reflections on whether the embedded theologies being expressed are life-giving or destructive at this moment in the crisis. They can ask questions such as these:

— Does her theology connect her with a compassionate loving God in moments when she condemns herself?
— Does his theology fully call him to account for the ways in which he has hurt others?
— Does her theology keep her so focused on herself that she loses sight of the needs of others? Does it help her love her neighbor as herself?
— Does his theology help him live out the promises he made when he joined a community of faith?
— Does her theology help her apprehend the mystery of God's presence in the midst of her crisis?

As shock and denial give way to a fuller awareness of a situation, people often shift into a modern mode, relying upon the expertise of medical and emergency personnel for definitive explanations based on science and technology. They may also be ready to engage in more deliberative theologizing about how they are experiencing God, what God wants for them, and how to understand their suffering. As pastoral caregivers engage in this deliberative theology with careseekers, they should assess the extent to which the emerging deliberative theology of the person in crisis reflects the fullness and mystery of God's being. In making such assessments, pastoral caregivers draw upon their theological education. They use biblical critical methods to interpret what biblical texts tell them about the careseeker's experience of God; they draw upon theological perspectives on evil and suffering to understand the careseeker's suffering. Using these sources and norms of authority, they engage in a process of coconstructing a deliberative theology with the careseeker. The more careseekers are able to tolerate the complexity and ambiguity of their suffering and God's presence, the more their deliberative theologies may include more radical reconstructions that take into account postmodern approaches to knowledge. Such reconstructions will become the basis for an enduring relationship with God, others, and self that can withstand the complexities and ambiguities of life in the twenty-first century.

When careseekers have moved through the acute phase of a crisis and are in the long-term phase of making sense theologically of their crisis, how can a pastoral caregiver and careseeker engage in deliberative theological reflection based upon postmodern approaches to knowledge? In answering this question, I turn first to a particular theological perspective described by Sheila Davaney in *Pragmatic Historicism: A Theology for the Twenty-first Century* (2000). Davaney describes this theology as a historicist enterprise that takes into account "the embodied, material, and political character of historical existence" (Davaney 2000, x) and the ways in which "we are inescapably shaped by our past, . . . [which] is not singular or univocal but always plural, consisting of multiple, diverse, and even conflicting elements" (Davaney 2000, 3). A historicist perspective views the context of pastoral care historically as "comprised of multiple, interacting processes—sociopolitical, economic, intellectual, religious, cultural, and so on—but these processes now can be seen more clearly to be both shaped by and the effective vehicles for the deployment of power" (Davaney 2000, 2). The task of historicism is to "construe the two dimensions of historical existence—our constitution by the past and our present context, and our agential capacity to create historical reality" (Davaney 2000, xii). Given this capacity to create historical reality, theologians using a historicist approach must become, in the end, pragmatic by developing strategies for social justice and healing.

Davaney's theology builds upon theologies that are trying to take into account postmodern uses of knowledge, pluralism, and complexity of life in the twenty-first century, and the forms that evil has taken in the twentieth and twenty-first centuries. Hers is a cross-disciplinary, postmodern theology that can "frame" pastoral care as it uses postmodern approaches to knowledge. Pastoral caregivers and theologians who understand suffering using postmodern theological approaches will appreciate Davaney's theology.

Postmodern approaches to theology incorporate a deep capacity for "theological empathy," by which I mean the ability to stand in the shoes of someone theologically different from us and appreciate how her theology can be a "home" for her in troubled, challenging times. Davaney's theology of "the embodied, material, and political character" of a careseeker's crisis is realized when a caregiver listens to a careseeker's story as if it were a novel that artistically renders the awful beauty of her life. Her theology is also realized when caregivers assess the ways in which the careseeker's cultural, community, and family systems ameliorate or intensify her suffering. Her theology challenges caregivers when they engage in theological reflection with careseekers, to coconstruct theologies that make sense of the complex ambiguities of their lives.

While Davaney provides an overarching frame for pastoral care that uses postmodern approaches to knowledge, caregivers need particular postmodern theological perspectives to do reflections that help them assess theologically how a careseeker makes sense of her suffering. I turn now to illustrating how a caregiver can employ a particular theological perspective as he or she approaches the step of engaging the careseeker in deliberative theology. I use two theological perspectives: Neville's (1996) theology of broken symbols and Poling's (1996) understanding of evil. I've chosen Neville and Poling for three reasons.

First, Neville's theology of broken symbols is contextually meaningful in the case studies that follow in this chapter and the next two chapters. It provides many rich ways of understanding (1) how people internalize and construct religious/existential symbols such that those symbols become an embedded theology, and (2) the extent to which these symbols may break and potentially be reconstructed when people go through crises or transitions. A potential liability of using Neville's theology of broken symbols is its focus on the individual and not his or her social context. To offset this liability, I will also use a theological perspective that focuses on issues of social identity and oppression: Poling's theology of evil as systemic abuse of power.

Second, both theologies are capable of engaging in a lively dialogue with the psychological and social identity theories discussed in chapters 5 and 6. Third, both theological perspectives can be used pragmatically to develop faith claims that serve as a theological basis for strategies seeking healing and justice.

A Theology of Broken Symbols

A central premise of Robert Neville's theology is that humans are part of a creation in which they are related to and conditioned by many other parts of creation. This creation is an interconnected finite system that owes its being to the unconditioned infinite, God, that sustains it. God cannot be known directly, and can be described only in the language of symbols, like Father, Mother, Creator, the Vine of Life, the Holy Spirit.

According to Neville, religious symbols are constructed on the boundary between finite creation and the unconditioned infinite and have to do with contrasts between the known and the unknown (Neville 1996, 47). Imagine standing at the top of a mountain that is one peak of a circular range. The valley below is life as we know it, the finite. When we turn around to look at the territory beyond this mountain range, the view is obscured and we cannot really see anything. This is the unconditioned infinite. When we describe experience and objects as having a sacred quality, these descriptions use symbolic language and are examples of "boundary markers between finite and infinite" (Neville 1996, 69). Consider, for example, a sculpture entitled *Christa,* by Edwina Sandys, which drew public attention in the late 1980s. It is in the form of a naked woman whose arms are outstretched as if she were nailed to a cross. For many viewers, the sculpture represents the suffering of female victims of violence. Its resemblance to Jesus' death on the cross conveys the meanings of this death and brings them to bear upon the particular suffering of violence. It represents, for example, the belief that God is profoundly present in the experience of violence and that nothing can separate victims from God's love.

Religious symbols arise out of the contexts of people's cultures and lives ("the biological, cultural, semiotic, and purposive nature of the interpreters" [Neville 1996, 241]). The sculpture *Christa,* for example, was created in a time when violence against women was receiving more and more public attention. Describing how such symbols function, Neville says, "When the symbols of a particular religious tradition are fresh and living, people see through them to the divine. They do not notice the symbols as such any more than they notice the glass in a window or think about columns of mercury when hearing the temperature from the TV weather announcer" (Neville 1996, 29).

The more a symbol reflects the changing contexts and lives of persons and communities, the more likely the symbol will change over

time. Those symbols no longer central to the faith experience of persons and/or communities may be set to the side or may need to be dramatically restructured so that they can portray new revelations of God.
Or people and communities may cling to symbols that are irrelevant or
so rigidly cast that they can never be broken by new revelations; these
symbols could, upon further analysis, be described as dead, like the
shell that remains when its living inhabitant is long gone. Trying to use
dead symbols to describe new revelations is like trying to store new
wine in old wineskins; the fermentation of the new wine breaks the
cracked, dried wineskin.

A pastoral caregiver using Neville's theology will first try to identify
the careseeker's symbol system. Although the entire conversation
between the caregiver and the person in crisis takes place on the boundary between the known and unknown, the careseeker may initially
deny the existential and religious nature of the crisis. A man, for example, who undergoes emergency cardiac bypass surgery may adopt the
attitude that his heart has been fixed and that he was never in any real
physical danger. Nonetheless, most careseekers in the face of a crisis will
explicitly speak from this boundary location, and in these moments
caregivers can glimpse the religious symbols they use to describe God.
Given that symbols have conscious and unconscious layers, and can be
multivalent in their depictions of ambiguous multiple experiences of
God, the pastoral caregiver will often feel like a sight-impaired person
grasping the elephant's trunk and describing a snake.

When I use novels or films as case studies, I am reminded of the
challenge for pastoral caregivers of gathering narrative fragments and
piecing together an understanding of the careseeker's use of religious
symbols. In many novels the reader is given information about how the
protagonist uses religious symbols. For example, in *The Secret Lives of
Bees* (Kidd 2002), fourteen-year-old Lily has a secret collection of items
that belonged to her dead mother and represent her mother's love. The
reader can appreciate how these items take on religious significance for
Lily, becoming part of the ritual ways in which she mourns her mother.
When, for example, she feels alone and unloved, she takes out her
mother's white gloves and strokes them. A youth minister, engaging
Lily in pastoral care, might never find out about these objects and what
they mean to Lily. Pastoral caregivers must listen to careseekers' stories
as if they were reading a well-written novel, and prompt the careseeker
to elaborate aspects of their stories that are hard to put into words.

Once the pastoral caregiver has started to identify the careseeker's religious symbols, the next step is to assess them theologically by asking three questions that Neville raises. First, to what extent is a careseeker able to interpret the symbols she uses? With this question, the pastoral caregiver is assessing whether the person in crisis is able to reflect on how she is making sense of things. Is she able to shift from using an embedded theology to becoming deliberative about her theology? Can she step back from the immediacy of the crisis, and reflect upon how she is experiencing God? In her conversations with a pastoral caregiver, is she able to engage in making sense of what has happened theologically? Using the concept of relational boundaries described in chapter 1, the caregiver can ask, is this person so merged in the crisis that she lacks any capacity for self-reflection? Or is this person so disengaged from the crisis that her reflections are intellectualized conjectures?

Second, what are the practical consequences of the careseeker's religious symbols? "Religious symbols deal with such basic matters as how we ought to live" (Neville 1996, 64), and this question concerns how symbols function in people's lives. The caregiver must ask, How does the use of a particular religious symbol help the careseeker cope in the midst of a crisis? How does it help with long-term meaning making? Will these religious symbols help the careseeker bear the weight of her suffering, like a well-constructed knapsack that holds all the provisions needed for a long trek? "Put in religious terms, the more divine matters are accurately grasped, the more people are transformed, enlightened or saved, at least within certain limits" (Neville 1996, 65). Take, for instance, the sculpture *Christa*, which conveyed a sense of God's presence to victims of violence who felt utterly alone in the experience of violence.

Third, what is the state of the careseeker's soul? What Neville calls the state of a person's soul, I prefer to understand contextually as arising out of a person's story and tradition. In order to discern a person's soul, the pastoral caregiver listens for how the careseeker refers to the sacred part of her life. For one person, for example, soul may be the sense of connection to the ancestors who spiritually inhabit the world around them. For another person, soul may be the experience of transcendence in which he and the world around him are transfigured with a divine presence. For others, soul may be the sense of oneness that comes when they worship with their religious community.

Case Study

The following case study illustrates how a pastoral caregiver can theologically reflect upon a careseeker's religious symbol system.

Judith Thomason is a Euro-American Presbyterian minister who has come to visit seventy-five-year-old Mrs. Rutter, also Euro-American, and a lifelong Presbyterian. She had breast cancer nearly fifteen years ago but had been given a clean bill of health after a mastectomy, chemotherapy, and regular checkups over a five-year period. She and her family have just found out that the nagging cough she has had for weeks is lung cancer and that cancer is throughout her body. Her physicians have told her and her family to arrange for hospice care. Mrs. Rutter has moved from her senior citizen apartment thirty-five miles away to her daughter Betsy's home, where a hospital bed has been installed in the ground floor guest room. Betsy is an active member of Knox Presbyterian Church, and she asked her mother if Betsy's minister, Judith Thomason, could visit, because a new interim minister has just arrived at Mrs. Rutter's church and doesn't know her. Judith Thomason has spoken with the interim minister, and they've agreed that Judith will do ongoing pastoral care and be available for a funeral.

This is the part of their initial conversation in which Mrs. Rutter and Judith Thomason talk about Mrs. Rutter's terminal illness.

> *Mrs. Rutter (1)*: I can't believe this is happening to me. You know that Beth [Betsy's twenty-six-year-old daughter] is supposed to get married in five weeks. It's so terrible that I've gotten sick right now. (She lowers her head, covers her face with her hand, and silently cries. Rev. Thomason briefly lays a hand gently on her shoulder. She cries for a few minutes, then sighs, reaches for a tissue and blows her nose.)
>
> *Rev. Thomason (1)*: This is such a hard time.
>
> *Mrs. Rutter (2)* (agitated): If only I could have just found out after the wedding was over. I should have just not gone to the doctor's office about that damned cough. I could have tried to get by.
>
> *Rev. Thomason (2)*: You wish that somehow you could have changed what's happening.
>
> *Mrs. Rutter (3)*: Yes, I go over and over the doctor's visit and keep thinking that I should have just waited. Then I end up saying to

God, please just let me get a little better, just for the next six weeks, so Betsy won't have to worry and look after me, and she can just focus on the wedding. If I could just stay strong enough to go to the wedding in a wheelchair . . . (She shakes her clenched hands and raises her voice.) O God, can't you just give me that? I want everything to be all right, just 'til the wedding.

Rev. Thomason (3): It sounds like you feel responsible for getting sick now.

Mrs. Rutter (4): Why did God do this to me?

Rev. Thomason (4): Why *did* God do this to you?

(Mrs. Rutter gives a deep sign, unclenches her hands, and her shoulders relax. She looks directly at Rev. Thomason.)

Mrs. Rutter (5): I'm so tired. I can't talk to Betsy about this. I just try to be strong when she's in the room. The pain is so bad at night. I don't want Betsy to know how bad it is.

Rev. Thomason (5): You're really trying to manage on your own right now.

Mrs. Rutter (6): I am. (She becomes tearful.) But it's not working. I don't know what to do. I feel like asking you to pray, but I don't really know what to pray for. I know that God isn't really making this happen to me. I don't know what to ask for.

Rev. Thomason (6): You need to ask for something?

Mrs. Rutter (7): I wish I could just let go, but I feel so responsible.

Rev. Thomason (7): Yes. Perhaps we could simply ask God to be with you right now.

Mrs. Rutter (8): Yes, could you pray for that? (She reaches out her hand and Judith takes it.)

Rev. Thomason (8): Loving God, be with us. Draw close to us in this moment. Be like the air we breathe, in and out; good air that helps us be close to you right now. (Rev. Thomason takes some deep breaths, and Mrs. Rutter does, too.) You are a light in the darkness, a candle burning bright. We can rest in you. We can let go. Whatever happens, you are with us. You are always with us. (Mrs. Rutter is breathing deeply. There is silence for a few minutes.)

Mrs. Rutter (9): O God, you have been so far away from me. (She becomes tearful.) I want you close. Help me stay close to you. You are so good.

Rev. Thomason (9): You are so good. Stay close.

Mrs. Rutter (10): Amen.

Rev. Thomason (10): Amen.

During this pastoral care conversation Judith glimpses Mrs. Rutter's religious symbol system in the various ways in which Mrs. Rutter describes her relationship with God. In moments of helplessness, she experiences God as all-powerful (*Mrs. Rutter [3]*): "God, please just let me get a little better, just for the next six weeks"; "O God, can't you just give me that?" In moments of anger she raises her voice in lament (*Mrs. Rutter [4]*): "Why did God do this to me?"

At other moments, she denies the reality of her terminal illness and the grief already experienced by her family. She envisions God as absent and herself as the one who should have been in control (*Mrs. Rutter [2]*): "If only I could have just found out after the wedding was over. I should have just not gone to the doctor's with that damned cough. I could have tried to get by." In replaying the memory of her doctor's visit, she imagines that she could have done something to prevent her illness occurring at this time. Her reaction is similar to traumatized persons who go over and over the memory of a car accident, imagining that if they had just turned the wheel in a different direction, or slammed on the brakes sooner, the accident could have been prevented.

Judith prompts Mrs. Rutter to be self-reflective when she echoes Mrs. Rutter's lament (*Mrs. Rutter [4]*), "Why did God do this to me?" In response to the question, Mrs. Rutter steps back from the immediacy of the lament, and experiences the weight of the burden she has been trying to carry (*Mrs. Rutter [4]*): "I'm so tired." She shifts to a deliberative theology (*Mrs. Rutter [6]*): "I know that God isn't really making this happen to me." She also acknowledges her sense of being overly responsible (*Mrs. Rutter [7]*): "I wish I could just let go, but I feel so responsible." In this moment, Mrs. Rutter demonstrates an ability to reflect upon her symbol system. She can look back at what she said about God making this happen to her. This ability to self-reflect is a turning point. Judith intervenes at this point, to see if Mrs. Rutter can experience God's presence.

What consequences follow Mrs. Rutter's experience of God with her? The immediate consequence in terms of this pastoral conversation is that she stops ruminating on the past and imaging God or herself as all-powerful. She also lets go of her obsessive focus on the future wedding and imaging God as absent and herself as isolated and responsible for everyone's happiness. She is able to be fully in the present moment, and bear the reality of her terminal illness because she now is connected with God, herself, and those, like Judith, who care for her. For someone approaching death, this ability to be connected and fully in the present moment is an enormous resource. Such connections will allow for a "safe" passage through her last days of life.

In this conversation, Judith senses that, for Mrs. Rutter, "soul" is this experience of being deeply connected and focused on the present moment. The centering prayer she uses with Mrs. Rutter "feeds her soul." In subsequent visits, she and Mrs. Rutter will experience other forms of spiritual nourishment, perhaps in the form of listening to sacred music, reading from Scripture, and receiving Communion.

Pastoral caregivers can use Neville's theology to explore and assess the meanings and roles of symbols in the stories, practices, and beliefs of people seeking care. A careseeker may be using religious symbols that have become irrelevant within the context of his life. Consider, for example, Jack, a young man who was raised as a Roman Catholic and has become a member of a Methodist congregation. When his best friend commits suicide, Jack, who lives two thousand miles away, wants to do something immediately in response to his friend's death. In agitation, he goes for a walk and comes to a Roman Catholic church. He enters, with the sudden thought that he could ask the priest to say a mass in memory of his dead friend. Then he remembers that his friend was not Roman Catholic. He realizes that his desire to have the priest celebrate a Eucharist in memory of his friend reflects childhood beliefs about the afterlife—some people's souls will not make it to heaven unless a number of religious rites are performed on their behalf. He ruefully acknowledges that, as an adult, he believes that Jack's soul is with God now. He doesn't need a religious rite to guarantee this.

When a religious symbol has great meaning for a careseeker, this meaning needs to be carefully explored, because sometimes symbols gain their life from participating in webs of violence, not webs of life. The symbol, for example, of Jesus suffering on the cross can convince people to remain in violent, life-threatening relationships. When symbols do participate in webs of life, they have the power to transform people's perspectives and practices. Pastoral caregivers must assess symbols in terms of their power to maintain webs of violence or webs of life, and to transform persons, families, and communities caught in webs of violence.

In doing a full assessment of Mrs. Rutter's social identity, Rev. Thomason must consider whether she experiences social advantages or disadvantages (see chapter 6) that affect her crisis of terminal illness. For example, she and her family have adequate financial resources, such that her terminal illness and home hospice care do not create financial stress. Her desire to conceal her illness in an effort to ensure the happiness of her granddaughter's wedding reflects her upbringing as a woman whose role it is to hold the family together. The way in which she was socialized as a wife and mother is, at least initially, a disadvantage. Judith Thomason also assesses whether the religious community and Mrs. Rutter's family are resources or roadblocks to her ability to cope with terminal illness. If there is no religious community to provide support for Mrs. Rutter and her daughter, they may find it more difficult to experience God's presence. If the family has a history of coping by focusing their energies in compulsive ways on external achievements, then they may deny Mrs. Rutter's terminal illness and compulsively prepare for a "perfect" wedding. If economic forces or family dynamics act in ways to dehumanize Mrs. Rutter near the end of her life, when she most needs to be loved and honored, then a theological perspective that highlights social and family oppression will be relevant to Mrs. Rutter's care. While many careseekers go through crises and transitions that simply have to do with loss, caregivers must consider the possibility of violence and oppression and the need for theological perspectives like Poling's theology of evil. I will summarize and then describe how his theology, used in dialogue with Neville's, can be relevant when a crisis has to do with violence and oppression.

Poling's Theology of Evil

Poling defines evil as the abuse of power and uses a systems perspective to describe three interconnected forms of evil: personal, social, and religious. "[E]vil [is] not only the discrete result of individual and social behaviors, but [is] also a complex web of power and violence that is carefully constructed over a long period of time and maintained through the actions and intentions of many individuals and groups"

(Poling 1996, 112). The ultimate consequences of evil are the destruction of bodies and spirits.

He contrasts evil with the loving power of life that comes from God, which is "characterized by sensitivity, the ability to internalize our relationship with others, and give value to the interconnectedness of the relational web" (Poling 1996, 114). Poling uses object-relations theory to describe how from early childhood on persons construct intrapyschic "maps" or matrices of their relational experiences of people that include, for example, images of self-mother, self-father, self-sibling relationships. A person also constructs images of God-self relationships that are often derived from significant relationships, like the relationship with father or mother (Rizzuto 1979). In the illustration involving Mrs. Rutter, at different moments she experiences God as angry and herself as fearful, God as absent and herself as needing to be in control, and God as loving and herself as trusting. These images become the experiential basis for Mrs. Rutter's symbols of God. In addition to an object-relations understanding of personality, Poling uses p[rocess theol]ogy to describe the interconnectedness of life as a web of [being. Like] relational matrix of images of self-other correspond to the e[xperience] life itself as a web of relationships.

Echoing Loomer's process theology of evil, Poling notes that "evil is not a foreign force outside of the life of bodies and spirits, but arises from life itself" (Poling 1996, 118). For example, conflict and power struggles are often part of intimate intense relationships in families between partners and between parents and children. In such power struggles, people often want to overpower the other, and in this process they easily treat the other as an object. Social systems, like family systems, also inevitably involve power struggles between those who have power and those who don't. The social need to categorize people, and the tendency to form stereotypes out of these categories, frequently results in the dehumanization of those who are different from oneself. Instead of treating each other as complex mysterious "subjects," people become objects. In psychological language, there is no intersubjectivity. In theological language, people no longer relate to each other as beloved children of God.

Evil is the result of sin, which is "the denial of loving sensitivity" and the "turning away from communion with self, others, and God" (Poling 1980, 95). Sin takes personal, social, and religious forms. "God has given us personal and social power for the purposes of enhancing value for individuals and for the relational web" (Poling 1996, 114). We sin when we abuse power and/or silently collude with an abuse of power. We also trespass on the inherent goodness of others and creation by treating both others and creation as objects.

The web of life is intertwined with the web of evil. The challenge for people of faith is that it can be difficult to distinguish whether they are using or experiencing power in a way that enhances the web of life or in a way that destroys it. While Poling asserts that abuse of power results in the destruction of spirits and bodies, he acknowledges how difficult it is to discern goodness from evil: "Evil is a chameleon that maintains itself by remaining intertwined with the good and masking itself as good" (119).

This intertwining of good and evil results in tragedy—the destruction of life and the web of life. Tragedy arises from three aspects of life. First, there isn't enough of the basic necessities of life for everyone, resulting in a conflict of goods—"the vital, integral dimensions of life," like "food, shelter, jobs, health, and political self-determination" (Sands 1994, 10, 11). As human beings, we inevitably face tragic conflicts in which someone will be hurt, no matter what choice we make. Given the interconnectedness of life, which using postmodern approaches we now can appreciate, tragic conflicts are part of life.[3] Second, we are created as human beings with freedom to choose between good and evil. Third, violence usually leads to more violence, generating intergenerational cycles of violence.[4]

Often it is only in historical retrospection that people can apprehend the evil that results in tragedy. An example is the practice in Canada and Australia of removing aboriginal children from their tribes and placing them in church-run boarding schools. The intention of the government and Christian organizations was to assimilate these children into Euro-American culture. The effect on these children and their families was devastating. Some of the children did not receive adequate food and medical attention; some were physically and sexually abused. They were forbidden from using their language, and their culture and religion were denigrated.

When confronted with evil like the kind I have just described, people of faith often feel compelled to make absolute truth claims. Kathleen Sands, a feminist postmodern theologian, argues cogently against making any absolute claims.

---

3. "In the postmodern moment, tragic conflicts do not just mark the borders of our lives but riddle them through and through" (Sands 1994, 6).

4. This three-part definition is from lecture notes by Larry Graham, from a course on theodicy and tragedy (Graham 2004).

The central issue at stake in the treatment of evil, I have argued, is what theology can and should do in a postmodern age. The question becomes especially pressing as theology draws more and more of its analyses of suffering and injustice from academic disciplines such as psychology, economics, and political theory. . . . Under those circumstances it can happen that the only distinctively theological part of the operation is also the part that has become least persuasive and perspicuous—the authorization of truth claims through appeal to an absolute referent. Fortunately, religion and spirituality have modes of meaning that are far more rich and subtle than that. It is in reflecting on these nonabsolute meanings, I propose, that theology can find its fullest role in the postmodern age . . . [turning] from idealized views of nature and the divine to the complex textures of mystical, aesthetic, and moral experience within particular historical communities.

(Sands 1

While pastoral caregivers should articulate truth claims in response to the tragic stories of violence told by careseekers, they must acknowledge that their claims are always contextual, constructed within a particular time and place. With this in mind, we turn to the faith claims proposed by Poling.

Poling's theology of evil is based upon these three faith claims: (1) God has given us life that we may use power for the goodness of creation, in ways that build a web of life. (2) As people of faith, we acknowledge that to participate in life fully will involve moments when we experience intense conflict and power struggles that can cause us to abuse power, that is, to sin and participate in sinful systems. (3) We live in an interconnected web of being in which we often cannot discern good from evil.

Pastoral caregivers are called to monitor power struggles and continually reflect upon the ways in which our use of power may be contributing to a web of violence. In Poling's words, we are called to "practice goodness" as "a form of faithfulness to the multiple, ambiguous life that comes when we follow Jesus" (Poling 1996, 175). Poling outlines strategies or behaviors for practicing goodness in the midst of violence, oppression, and evil:

— Develop a spirituality of resistance.
— Live in solidarity with resistance communities.
— Take moral and material inventory.

— Confront the abuser within.
— Confront persons of power.
— Negotiate with institutions.

Combining Poling's theology of evil, resistance, and the multivalency and ambiguity of God with Neville's theology of broken symbols creates a rich, multifaceted theological understanding for pastoral caregivers who engage in deliberative theology with careseekers.

EXERCISE 7: THEOLOGICAL REFLECTION

Review your verbatim, and highlight anything the careseeker says or implies about her religious/spiritual beliefs, practices, or images of God. Review the highlighted material several times and see if you can identify the themes around which her statements cluster. Examples of such themes are suffering—especially grief and anger; images/experience of God or that which is experienced as sacred (like nature, beauty, art); sin/guilt/shame, despair/hope concerning what is happening to her now and what will happen in the future; death and the afterlife (ultimate separation, spiritual connections with those who have died). Consider also any theme that is relevant to the careseeker's experience, even though such themes were not part of the verbatim.

1. Describe each theme by identifying the statements that the careseeker makes which explicitly or implicitly refer to this theme.
2. Theologically assess the careseeker's beliefs, practices, and experiences of God/the sacred by answering the following questions that make use of Neville's theology of religious symbols:

   — Does the careseeker seem to have the capacity to deliberate or reflect critically upon these religious beliefs, practices, experiences, and symbols of God?
   — What are the practical consequences of the careseeker's religious beliefs, practices, experiences, and symbols of God? How do these beliefs, practices, experiences, and symbols of God help the careseeker cope in the midst of a crisis? How do they help with long-term meaning-making? Will these religious beliefs, practices, experiences, and symbols of God help the careseeker bear the weight of her suffering?

— What is the state of the careseeker's soul? Think about how you understand the term "soul" contextually in terms of the careseeker's story and tradition. Listen for how the careseeker refers to the sacred part of her life.

3. Use Poling's theological perspective to answer these questions:

— Are the careseeker's beliefs, practices, experiences, and symbols of God part of a web of life (think about what you wrote in reply to question 2 about the consequences of the careseeker's beliefs, practices, experiences, and symbols of God)?
— Are they part of a web of violence?

8

Plans of Care: Seeking Healing and Justice

After the caregiver has listened to the careseeker's story—reflecting upon themes of loss and violence, reviewing her ways of coping, and assessing the impact of cultural, community, and family systems—and engaged in theological reflection, the caregiver is ready to formulate a plan of care to address the needs of the careseeker and, if necessary, her family, communities, and cultural system. The goal is not only the transformation of persons, but also the families, communities, and cultures forming the web of relationships that supports them. Caregivers must recognize that certain aspects of social identity, such as class and gender, may result in oppression, and in the face of continuing abuses of power, healing of persons may not be ultimately possible. In that case, the strategies for practicing goodness outlined by Poling (chapter 7) can become part of a plan of care.

The plan of care described in this chapter has three steps: (1) attending to the careseeker's safety and building trust, (2) mourning losses, and (3) reconnecting with life.[1] These steps form a plan of care to be used for those who are in crisis or transition and whose narratives include themes of loss, violence, and compulsive ways of coping.

---

1. These steps reflect the work of Herman (1992) and Fortune (1987, especially in Fortune's work as the director of the Center for the Prevention of Sexual and Domestic Violence in Seattle).

Step 1: Attend to the Careseeker's Safety and Build Trust

To seek the safety of the careseeker must be the most immediate concern for pastoral caregivers who determine someone is experiencing violence, and caregivers can do this in several ways. First, as noted in chapter 4, many state and provincial laws now require ministers to report their suspicions that children, teenagers, elders, and the disabled are being sexually, physically, and psychologically abused or neglected. The purpose of these laws is to guarantee that an immediate assessment of danger is done by those with appropriate expertise, namely, social workers and/or law enforcement officers, who can if necessary take action to ensure the safety of a victim.

Thus, when caregivers find out that a child, teenager, elderly, or disabled person is in danger, they must consult with ecclesial and legal counsel about whether they are mandated reporters in their state and also whether their denominational code of conduct requires them to report abuse (see chapter 4). Whether or not they are mandated reporters, they can encourage victims to report the abuse themselves. Taking such action can enhance a victim's sense of self-agency and become a step in the process toward recovery.

When caregivers discover that an adult careseeker is a victim of violence, they review with the victim all options available to her or him, like contacting a rape crisis center or a shelter for victims of domestic violence, going to an emergency room if there are physical injuries, and reporting the crime to the police. While they need to encourage victims to seek safety and report crimes, they must also respect a victim's right to decide for him or herself what further action, if any, to take. Empowering victims, not arresting offenders, is the immediate goal of care.

When careseekers contact caregivers while violence is occurring—by phoning, for example, when an attack is under way—caregivers must call the police immediately and not try to intervene themselves in what are often highly dangerous and explosive scenarios. The police are the only ones equipped to respond in the midst of violence.

A second way in which caregivers must attend to the safety of the careseeker is by asking questions about suicidality (see chapter 5). When a careseeker in acute grief expresses a sense of despair, for example, the caregiver must ask whether he ever has thoughts of ending his life. A man, for instance, who is extremely dependent on his wife may become suicidal when she announces that she has a lover and abruptly leaves. Adolescents experiencing a crisis because of their growing realization that they are gay, lesbian, or transgender may become suicidal. A mother who is experiencing postpartum depression may consider suicide as the only way out of the dark hole in which she is caught.

After the caregiver has determined that the careseeker is physically safe from harm by asking about violence and suicidality, reporting abuse if so required, and reviewing options with adult victims, he or she can assess the disorganizing and chaotic effects of the person's acute grief, reactions to violence, or use of compulsive ways of coping. With the careseeker, and perhaps with members of the person's caregiving team, the caregiver can develop daily strategies for helping the careseeker cope with his or her intense psychological, spiritual, and relational responses to crises. They can explore, for example, what will help the careseeker regain a sense of calm. Religious and spiritual practices like prayer, worship, Christian sacraments, reading Hebrew and Christian Scriptures, and listening to music may help the careseeker find moments of peace and the strength to engage in the daily routines necessary for life. When a careseeker can effectively use spiritual and religious practices to cope with stress during the acute stage of a crisis, such coping will become an ongoing resource in maintaining and deepening a connection with God and a sense of life as sacred.

Caregivers cannot assume, however, that all religious and spiritual practices are life-giving. A careseeker who has psychological tendencies to become obsessive in a crisis may use prayer in ways that actually increase his anxiety. Someone who uses the practice of confession to reconnect with God because she feels a profound sense of guilt about having an abortion may continue to experience guilt in spite of her spiritual practices. In that case, she will need to explore the nature of her guilt with her pastor, for simply returning over and over to a sacrament that is not helping her reconnect with God, that might even be deepening the disconnection, is not a life-giving spiritual practice.

A woman in a violent marriage may feel responsible for the well-being of the marriage and cope by accepting patriarchal aspects of her religious tradition, trying harder to be the kind of "good wife" described in the book of Proverbs. She may believe that her husband's violence is the cross she has to bear, or even a punishment from God.[2] She may feel mandated by Scripture to forgive her husband when he is remorseful. She may not tell anyone about the violence or how she

---

2. Empirical studies of how people use religions to cope with stress have demonstrated that persons of faith who understand negative events as a punishment from God are likely to experience poorer psychological outcome (Pargament 1997, 288).

understands it in terms of her religious beliefs, because of shame and fear. Such uses of religious sources and norms of authority perpetuate the cycle of violence. Similarly, a single person may struggle with whether and how to explore her sexual compatibility with a potential partner. She may prematurely adopt a simplistic theological understanding of purity and the Holiness Codes described in the book of Leviticus, codes which culturally functioned then, as they do now in the culture wars of the United States, as a response of a religious nation under threat.[3]

When a caregiver determines that a careseeker's religious practices are harmful, he or she can first ask the careseeker about the immediate effects of engaging in the practice: Does the careseeker feel peaceful, comforted, or hopeful? How long does this feeling last? A careseeker who invokes or defers to an all-powerful God may feel a sense of calm in the crisis; however, these images of God and self may become harmful when it is time for the careseeker to assume a greater sense of self-agency and experience God in a collaborative relationship, as part of a web of being.[4] When a caregiver explores with a careseeker the effect of her spiritual practice, she may recognize that these effects do not last long and may make the recurrence of a problem—violence, intense guilt, shame, fear—even more disturbing. The next step is considering alternate religious practices and seeing if the careseeker is willing to try any of them. During this process, it is important for the caregiver to respect the careseeker's need for familiar, if harmful, practices and beliefs that have been his or her only way of spiritually surviving thus far. Caution must be exercised in suggesting that a careseeker abandon harmful religious practices before new ones have become meaningful. Caregivers may need to be patient and provide ongoing support until careseekers are ready to let go of harmful practices.

In addition to assessing whether a person's spiritual practices are harmful, caregivers can also assess whether such practices are based on a theology that can provide sufficient meaning, given the tragic conflicts—described in chapter 7—that so often are experienced in a crisis. Like reinforced steel that is strong enough to bear the weight of a building, theological ways of understanding suffering must be strong enough

---

3. "When the body of a society is threatened, part of the response is to take great care over the unity, purity and integrity of the human body. The ancient Israelites were certainly under threat a great deal. The Holiness Code, which dates from the period after the exile when Israel was disillusioned and despondent, seeks to unite and rebuild the nation as a distinct and whole entity" (Stuart and Thatcher 1997, 91).

4. In Pargament's (1997) empirical research on how people use religion to cope with stress, he found three styles of coping: self-directing, collaborative, and deferring. The collaborative style is most consistently correlated with psychological health.

to bear the weight of the careseeker's suffering. When a religious practice is rooted in a simplistic theology, while it may help a person reestablish a sense of trust in God during the most intense moments of crisis, it may not, in the long run, be able to help her fully name the extent of her suffering and construct meanings that allow for a full grieving of irrevocable losses. As I have noted elsewhere, in the height of a crisis the role of religion and spirituality can be likened to how religion was used in premodern times, when absolute belief in God was the only hope of surviving life's often insurmountable suffering. Reestablishing a person's basic trust in God and finding intrinsic religious meanings are challenging in a postmodern age.

While the pastoral caregiver may initially focus on the individual careseeker in attending to the careseeker's safety and building a sense of trust, she will also want to assess whether the careseeker's most intimate relationships, family, community, and culture ameliorate or exacerbate the acute stage of a crisis (see chapter 6). If the crisis involves relational tensions and conflicts in intimate relationships and families, then strategies for surviving the most acute effects of the crisis need to take these relationships into account. Such strategies will consist of finding ways to lower the intensity of emotional reactivity and, if possible, to allow those involved to reexperience a basic sense of connection with each other. Any strategy that helps those in conflict regain "neutral ground" is helpful; by this I mean, finding strategies that couples can use to defuse emotional reactivity, gain emotional space, and enjoy shared activities. For example, when a crisis causes intense conflict between a parent and an adolescent son or daughter, the caregiver can strategize with one or the other, or preferably both, about whether there may be times together, like going to school in the car, which can be declared a "no war" zone.

If a crisis is exacerbated by being with intimate partners or friends, family, or in particular communities, or by being exposed to certain aspects of one's culture, then caregiver and careseeker can think about strategies so that these relational systems are not allowed to intensify their suffering. Poling (1996) calls such strategies resisting abuses of power. Maintaining more emotional distance can be helpful for someone who has an overinvolved anxious or critical parent. Finding alternative ways of relaxing and socializing when one's friends abuse alcohol may be a necessary strategy for those who use alcohol excessively to cope with stress. Developing strategies for surviving in a homophobic environment until a person is able to leave the environment or changes can be made may be a focus of care for those experiencing crises associated with their lesbian or gay sexual identities.

When one's intimate relationships, families, communities, and culture are resources, then the caregiver and careseeker can strategize on how to use these resources more fully. Pastoral caregivers can focus on resources that deepen a connection with God and the sense of life as sacred. Careseekers can be intentional about seeking out relationships and activities that are affirming.

Communal spiritual and religious practices can be intensely meaningful for those in the acute stage of a crisis. Religious rituals can help a careseeker experience the immediacy of the presence of God and the community of faith. Going to celebrations of the Eucharist can sustain a careseeker who is having difficulty getting through each day. The sensations of tasting the bread and wine in the sacrament of Communion can help a careseeker experience a sense of God's presence within her. By meditating on the stations of the cross—depictions of the suffering Jesus experienced in the final hours of his life—a careseeker can apprehend how her story of suffering is contained within the story of the suffering of Jesus. The familiar rhythm of saying the prayers of the rosary or lighting a candle in a church sanctuary in remembrance of a loved one can be comforting.

As the caregiver listens for themes of violence, loss, and coping in a careseeker's story; explores whether his culture, community, and family are helping him or getting in the way; inquires about spiritual practices and beliefs; and explores together which religious strategies help, a relationship of trust is formed. A careseeker will have the sense of being fully heard when a caregiver attends to the details of her story. By inquiring about how she is coping and exploring new strategies, a caregiver conveys a sense of being with a careseeker in her daily struggles. When caregivers learn the ways in which a careseeker makes sense of her crisis in terms of her faith and then coconstructs with her a language with which to talk about God, a relationship of trust is further deepened. The careseeker is ready for the emotional and spiritual work of mourning losses.

Step 2: Mourn Losses

Once the acute effects of a crisis—the sense of disorganization and chaos, the overwhelming emotional reactions, and the debilitating physical impact on sleeping, eating, and working—subside, the care-giver can focus on helping the careseeker mourn the losses, if any, incurred in the crisis. When the crisis involves a loss—like retirement, the end of a relationship, or ongoing health impairments—careseekers need space and time to mourn. Caregiving involves constructing mean-ings and practices that can deepen a sense of connection with God and the web of being that includes self, others, and all of creation. As described in chapter 5, psychologies describing reconstruction of meaning systems can be used in dialogue with theolog not only to come to terms with suffering, but to expe ultimately as a redemptive source of revelation.

During this phase of care, pastoral care will take many forms. It will not likely involve the weekly meetings that were part of crisis interven-tion. Meeting weekly after the acute stage of a crisis has subsided puts caregivers at risk of functioning as psychotherapists. The focus of pas-toral care at this point is on the religious and spiritual dimensions of coming to terms with change, and care should include many aspects of religious and spiritual life: individual spiritual practices, communal worship, exploration of religious and spiritual meanings through Bible study or faith-based discussion groups involving reading and reflecting upon religious sources and norms of authority. These aspects of spiri-tual and religious life can help the careseeker fully experience and explore the meanings of his or her suffering, experience a sense of God and the sacred in this process, and become more deeply embedded in a web of being.

The time it takes people to mourn varies from person to person, depending on (1) the severity of the loss or violence, (2) whether there is a history of violence and/or unmourned losses, (3) whether psycho-logical vulnerabilities to depression, anxiety, or other forms of mental illness are exacerbated, and (4) whether there is family and community support. Many people need one year because on important anniversary dates they will reexperience acute grief. Once a year has passed, their emotional responses to reminders and anniversaries of the crisis will not be so intense. A person who has had time to grieve will feel sadness in response to reminders, and such sadness will foster a sense of connec-tion with her self, God, and what has been lost.

The pastoral caregiver is a guide in this process of religious and spiri-tual meaning making. In this capacity, caregivers not only attend to how the careseeker is mourning losses and coming to terms with change; the caregiver will help the careseeker reflect upon the continuing role of intimate relationships, family, communities, and cultures in supporting or blocking the healing process. According to a systems perspective of the embeddedness of persons within relationships, families, communities, and culture, change to individuals inevitably involves change within that person's relational network. Sometimes amazing transformations of intimate relationships, families, and communities come about because of personal transformation. Those who experience profound transformation through their religious and spiritual lives can bring about family, community, and social change; Mother Teresa, Martin Luther King Jr., Henri Nouwen, and Dietrich Bonhoeffer are persons whose transformed lives brought forth radical changes in the world around them. In stark contrast are the tragic stories, with which we are all familiar, of those ultimately destroyed by their suffering and the abuses of power that break their bodies and their spirits, found in daily news reports of a child murdered by one of her parents, a woman killed by her ex-lover, a young adult who commits suicide.

As one concerned with the care of persons, the pastoral caregiver can consider the ways in which relational systems support grieving losses and ending violence in relationships. She can support social justice ministries in the congregation, her denomination, and her neighborhood. She can become affiliated with parent education programs, rape crisis centers, and shelters for battered women. She can address issues of racism, sexism, and homophobia in her sermons. Such activities can instill a sense of hope in caregivers who provide care to persons caught in violent relationships or addictions.

Step 3: Reconnect with the Ordinariness of Life

The final step of care is reconnecting with the goodness of life. Moments of reconnection happen throughout a crisis and may be especially vivid and empowering in the darkest moments of acute stress. Raymond Carver's story "A Small, Good Thing" (1988) depicts such a moment, when parents, enraged by the death of their son, encounter the baker who has been pestering them with anonymous phone calls after they failed to pick up their son's birthday cake on the day he died. When they finally realize who has been making these calls, they drive to the bakery before the sun has risen and storm in to confront the baker. After bearing the brunt of their rage, the baker coaxes them to sit down and eat some freshly baked bread, saying, "Eating is a small, good thing in a time like this" (Carver 1988, 301).

One feature of such moments of reconnection is the sense of being fully present in the immediate moment, without it being overshadowed by losses from the past or fears about the future. Such moments can allow both pastoral caregivers and careseekers to experience a sense of God's presence and the sacredness of life. When either the caregiver or careseeker recognizes and identifies the religious and spiritual meanings of such moments, they become even more life giving; some theologically interpret such moments as glimpses of eternal life or epiphanies— manifestations of God. Religious symbols and meanings systems offer deep and rich images of such moments of connecting with the goodness of life. Artistic language can often convey the beauty of these moments. Moral language can cast into sharp relief issues of accountability and justice.

Moments of connecting with the goodness of life can accumulate when careseekers fully mourn their losses and face their experiences of violence. Indeed, a central goal of pastoral care is deepening this connection with the goodness of life, and resisting and challenging all that threatens and destroys life. One of the roles of the caregiver is to help the careseeker recognize and cherish such moments and find strategies to experience them increasingly.

In this last phase of care, careseekers will have less and less need for contact with a caregiver, because they will gradually gain a sense of spiritual connection with all that is good in their lives.

EXERCISE 8: PLANNING CARE

Use the following categories and questions to develop a written plan of care for the person in your verbatim.

1. Attending to the careseeker's safety, building trust

— Is safety an issue for the careseeker? Is she or he experiencing sexual, physical, or psychological violence? If so, what steps can be taken to ensure that she or he is safe?

— Are there moments in the verbatim when it seems as though the careseeker is gaining a sense of trust in you? What can you do to ensure that this trust deepens?

2. Mourning losses

— What will the careseeker need if she or he is coping with the acute experience of grief? How can her or his religious and spiritual life be a resource to her or him?

— As her or his acute grief begins to subside, what will help her or him come to terms with these losses over the long term? Think about available religious and spiritual resources and consider what might help him or her connect with a sense of the sacred.

— How can his or her community of faith support him or her in mourning losses?

3. Reconnecting with the ordinary goodness of life

— Is there evidence in your pastoral care conversation that the careseeker has moments of experiencing the ordinary goodness of life?

— How can you and he or she be aware of such moments and celebrate them when they come along?

9
Affliction: *A Case Study*

Chapters 1 to 8 described each step of pastoral care. It is now time to put these steps together and illustrate care that moves from listening; to assessing losses, violence, coping, and cultural, community, and family systems; and then to reflecting theologically and planning care. In this chapter, I use Russell Banks's novel *Affliction* (from which the quotes are taken), as well as the film version directed by Paul Schrader (Largo Enterprises, 1998), as a case study to describe how a minister can provide pastoral care to someone in crisis, in this case, forty-one-year-old Wade Whitehouse, who is both violent and alcoholic.[1] The story is told by Wade's brother Rolfe, who is trying to understand what went wrong in the weeks before Wade disappeared after killing his father, setting the farmhouse on fire, and murdering a co-worker.

We will begin partway through the story, with a scene at the family's New Hampshire farmhouse. The Whitehouse family has gathered there just before the funeral of Wade's elderly mother, Sally Whitehouse, who froze to death because her husband, Glenn, in his drunkenness did not realize how cold the house had become after the furnace broke down. Gathered at the farmhouse are Glenn, Wade the eldest son, his fiancée Margie, Wade's sister Lena, Lena's husband Clyde, Wade's youngest brother Rolfe, Rev. Doughty, a mortician, and a family friend.

1. The story depicted in the film will be described for readers. To gain the most from this chapter, readers can watch the film, and cast themselves into the role of pastoral caregiver.

143

Everyone is sitting awkwardly in a circle except for Wade and Glenn, who move around the room restlessly, getting one drink after another. Clyde stands up and announces that he will lead them in prayer. He drops to his knees and begins a fervent prayer, which Lena punctuates with exclamations of "Praise the Lord!" The rest of the family, not evangelical conservative Christians, hastily kneel. During the lengthy prayer, Glenn, sitting alone in a corner, becomes agitated. He walks away from the group and pours himself a shot of whiskey. Then he steps into the middle of the circle and shouts, "Not one of you is worth a Goddamned hair on that good woman's head" (Banks 1989, 228).

Rev. Doughty leaves the room with the mortician, saying, "This is a difficult time. . . . Emotions run high at a time like this" (Banks 1989, 228). Each of the adult children reacts to their father's violence as they did when they were children: Rolfe, for example, hangs his head in shame and backs away. When Lena tentatively asks her father to get rid of the demons by giving himself to Jesus, he curses her and she recoils as if struck. Wade, the eldest son, takes on his father physically. His father shouts vindictive insults and strikes out at Wade's fiancée Margie, who tries to intervene. Wade forces his father against the wall and threatens to kill him if he ever hits Margie again. At this point, the mortician opens the door from the porch, announcing that it is time to leave for church. The minister has gone ahead.

In this scene, the minister witnesses an episode of family violence and does not take action by calling the police. Given the likely presence of firearms in the house, he should intervene quickly before violence escalates. He also does not subsequently consult with denominational representatives and local social services to see if he is a mandatory reporter of elder abuse. He has no further contact with Wade or his father, even though he no doubt hears that Wade continues to drink and becomes increasingly violent at work. He does not assess the likelihood of future violence for elderly Mr. Whitehouse, Margie, or Wade's daughter when she visits.

Let's imagine what could happen if the steps presented in this book were followed. To begin, we return to the family scene at the farmhouse. Instead of stepping outside of the room when violence erupts, the male minister I describe below begins a pastoral care relationship with this family. From this point to the end of the chapter, I will describe a fictional minister who provides the best care he can. He has probably been asked to preside over this funeral because of historical connections between this family and the church. He knows Glenn,

Wade, and Margie, who are all local. He may know something about the family through conversations with church members. He's heard that Glenn Whitehouse has always been an alcoholic husband who beat his wife and children. He knows that Sally froze to death three days ago while Glenn was in a drunken stupor. What sort of ministry can he provide for this family? His first task is to assess whether there are any immediate risks.

Assessing Immediate Risks

At the farmhouse, there is a risk of violence quickly escalating. As a professional trained to recognize family violence and to take steps in such an emergency, the minister must remain in the room with the family and be prepared to call the police if Wade and his father start throwing punches. While there are enough men to separate Wade and Glenn physically, no one knows if Wade, as the town's parttime sheriff, has a gun with him or if Glenn has one in the house.

Immediately following the funeral, the minister must find out whether he is mandated to report the elder abuse he witnessed, by consulting his denominational representatives and local social services. Given that he witnessed the violence himself, and it was not reported to him in a pastoral care conversation that could be legally considered privileged communication, he likely is required legally and ethically to report the abuse, so that local social services can assess whether it is safe for Glenn to live by himself in the farmhouse, and also whether there is further risk of violence if Wade becomes his caretaker. In assessing these risks, the minister is putting into action a plan of care whose first goal is to attend to Glenn's safety.

The minister next arranges to meet with the family after the funeral. His first meeting is with Wade, who has asked Margie to come along. Wade arrives looking somewhat disheveled. There is alcohol on his breath and he continually rubs his jaw, reporting that he has a toothache and hasn't been able to get to a dentist. Wade talks excitedly about his plans to move into the farmhouse with Margie and fight for legal custody of Jill, his daughter from his marriage to Lillian. Margie expresses concern about how they will manage financially, because Wade has just been fired from both his parttime jobs, as sheriff and as driver of one of the town's snowplows. When the minister explores what happened at work, Wade excitedly tells a story about a confrontation he had with a co-worker, Jack, which resulted in an accident that ruined his boss's car. At this point, the minister realizes that Wade is in crisis: he is dysfunctional at work, abusing alcohol, and becoming violent with increasing frequency. In this precarious psychological state, he is about to set up a new household with his fiancée and daughter. After their hourlong conversation, the minister has enough information about the volatile state Wade is in to know that crisis intervention is needed.

The minister must assess further Wade's losses, experiences of violence, and his use of alcohol to cope with stress.

Assessing Losses

As the minister listens to Wade's story, he first considers whether Wade is experiencing grief over his mother's death. Wade does not initially say anything about no longer being able to relate to her through conversations, touch, and physical presence. This absence—or perhaps denial—of grief immediately after the funeral surprises the minister, given the sudden and shocking circumstances of her death. Knowing that Wade's mother died of neglect and that she was said to have been physically abused by her husband in the past, Rev. Doughty wonders whether Wade's lack of grief may be because, for Wade, his mother as a person outside of her family roles disappeared long ago, obliterated by her husband's violence and brutality. Wade's disorganization and inability to regulate his intense anger and reactions are evidence of the unconscious effects of grief on him. For Wade, two conscious feelings exist: numbness and anger. He doesn't seem to feel any of the usual feelings that are part of grief, such as emptiness, loneliness, anxiety, guilt, shame, and sadness (Mitchell and Anderson 1983, 61).

The minister, judging that Wade is not able to recognize, let alone mourn, the profound losses he has experienced, will set aside, for the time being, the goal of helping Wade mourn his losses. Instead, he will pay attention to Wade's present emotional state involving his excitement about (1) events at work concerning his young co-worker Jack, and (2) moving to the farmhouse with Margie and having his daughter Jill stay with them.

Before ending the conversation, the minister asks Wade to step outside for a moment while he talks with Margie. When he and Margie are alone, he asks her if Wade has ever become physically violent with her. Margie assures him that he hasn't and expresses concern about Wade's relationship with his father. The minister asks her whether she has thought about what she would do if Wade did become violent with her or with his father, as he did at the farmhouse. Margie is not sure. He urges her to be prepared to leave immediately, call the police, and go somewhere safe. He gives her a pamphlet describing a local shelter for battered women.

He next asks Wade to rejoin them and tells him that he has contacted the local social services because of his concern about his father's safety. Wade is angry and wants to know what is going to happen next. The minister reports that a team of social workers is going to the farmhouse today and that they will arrange to meet with Wade later on. Margie expresses relief that Mr. Whitehouse is being evaluated. Wade grudgingly admits this might be a good idea, acknowledging that his father hasn't been to a physician for years. The minister suggests that they meet in a few days, and at Margie's urging, Wade agrees to return.

What follows is a verbatim of their next conversation.

Minister (1): Wade, I realized today that it was just one week ago when you called me from the farmhouse to arrange the funeral. How are you feeling about your mother's death?

Wade (1): It was too bad about Mom. Pop just didn't know how to look after her. I saw my lawyer yesterday. I was telling him that the custody case is going to be stronger now that I can bring Jill to the farmhouse.

Minister (2): What was it like growing up on the farm?

Wade (2): It was rough. There was never enough money, and life was hard. (He shakes his head.) I want to fix up the house. Margie can help clean things up and make it a decent place to raise Jill.

Minister (3): I'm surprised to hear about these plans. You must have been thinking about the farmhouse even before your mother died.

Wade (3): Heck, I should have thought about this a long time ago. I never realized that Pop couldn't look after Mom. She shouldn't have died like that. It's time for me to look after the rest of the family.

Minister (4): I wonder if your mother's death made you realize how important your family is. You're trying to bring the family together in a new way at the farmhouse. It sounds to me like you're trying to right the wrongs of the past, in particular, your father's neglect of his mother.

Wade (4) (laughs): You sound just like my brother Rolfe. He's always trying to figure out what's going on in my head. Hell, I don't even know what's going on.

Minister (5): Is that something you want to know more about?

Wade: (5): No. I just want to get on with my plans.

Minister (6): I'm concerned about you, Wade. I know you've been drinking today because I can smell beer on your breath. I've seen how angry you can get. You were ready to hit your father at the farmhouse last week. I know there's been trouble at work. I think you need to talk to a social worker or a psychologist, someone who can help you understand what's going on before you hurt yourself or someone else.

Wade (6): I'm fine. I'll be okay. I don't want to talk to anyone right now. (He gets up, heading for the door.)

Minister (7): I'd like to phone in a few days and see how you're doing.

Wade (7): Okay. I'm going to be pretty busy. I have a lot of things to look after.

Because he realizes there is a lot going on that he doesn't understand, the minister begins to check in with Wade every three days, a plan of care that is warranted by the intensity of the crisis that Wade is in. He also senses that many people are at risk: Wade is drinking, is often angry, and has been using physical force with his father, co-worker, and boss.

Over the next several weeks, as Wade begins to trust the minister, he describes a hunting accident in which a businessman shot himself while with Wade's co-worker Jack. Wade is suspicious of this death, and wonders aloud with the minister whether Jack is involved in some sort of real estate scheme. Wade's conjectures about the hunting accident and a real estate scheme don't make sense to the minister, but he is most struck by Wade's apparent obsession with Jack. He realizes that he doesn't have the psychological knowledge and skills to assess this obsession, and that Wade needs psychological care. The minister knows that Wade has had many losses in his life, that he has used alcohol and violence as ways of coping with stress, and that the stress he is presently experiencing has put him into an almost manic state of excitement. The minister must try once again to refer Wade to a psychologist as soon as possible to assess what is going on.

If in the novel the minister had been able to convince Wade to see a psychologist, and the psychologist had met with Wade for several intake sessions, this story would have emerged: a story about loss, violence, alcoholism, and social oppression, as we will see.

The roots of Wade's obsession with his co-worker Jack lie in both the story of Wade's marriage to Lillian and the violence he experienced when he was growing up. The story of his first marriage is heart-wrenchingly sad. He and Lillian had been high school sweethearts. Wade cherished this relationship's moments of intimacy that brought out qualities of tenderness and intelligence that he had never felt or acted on before. In such moments, he was no longer like the men around him, "deliberately roughened and coarse, cultivating their violence for one another to admire and shrink from, growing up with a defensive willed stupidity and then encouraging their sons to follow" (Banks 1989, 300).

When Wade graduated from high school, he married Lillian and worked full time. But then things changed. Banks describes his reactions to all of the adult roles he assumed with that marriage:

> [H]ere he was, living like a trapped adult, a man much older than he, a man whose life was already determined in every important way—by the job at LaRiviere's, by the small dark apartment itself, filled with other people's castoffs, by the village of Lawford itself, all of it hemmed in by the dark hills and forests. This was adult life, and he was not ready to accept it.
>
> He had started to drink heavily, usually at Toby's after work, and had grown confused and angry. And he quickly lost his connection to that lovely young thing, the fragile humorous affection for the world that he had nurtured and kept alive all through adolescence, and he grew increasingly angry at the loss and began to blame Lillian for it. The more he blamed her, the further he flew from it, until, indeed, he *was* like the men who surrounded him, and one night he lashed out at her with his fists and afterwards wept in her lap, begging forgiveness, promising to be different, new, clean, loving, gentle, funny.
>
> But within weeks, he found himself breaking his promise, horrifying himself, and he began to blame the context of his madness, his life with Lillian, confusing it with the cause of his madness, and so he left her.
>
> (Banks 1989, 302)

The intrapsychic loss of the tenderness and intelligence he had experienced with Lillian is a disenfranchised loss (Doka 1989; Karaban 2000), that is, a loss for which one cannot grieve publicly for fear of shame or judgment. He could not acknowledge it because he would have been ridiculed by the men in his community, especially his father. Wade himself could not name and mourn this loss and coped by drinking and becoming violent.

Assessing Violence

As a child and teenager, Wade protected his mother and siblings by becoming the target of his father's violence. When Glenn beat his sons, he shouted demeaning insults, calling them "sissies" and "candy-asses." As an adult, Wade had flashbacks to his childhood experiences of violence. One such flashback occurred right after he talked to Margie about getting married. Wade could not talk about these flashbacks, in spite of the fragile intimacy he had with Margie. The physical and psychological abuse he experienced as a child was still too shameful (Ramsay 1991) to be shared and needed to be hidden.

The patterns of violence in Wade's childhood resulted in traumatization, along with intense psychological longings and needs he still experienced in adult life. Often, when children are neglected (Pattison 1998) and abused as Wade was, they have great difficulty learning to regulate intense feelings (Linehan 1993) and may alternate between being overpowered by these feelings, so that they act impulsively, and becoming emotionally numb. Another psychological consequence of Wade's childhood experiences of violence was the formation in childhood and adolescence of neurological pathways signaling danger and a heightened arousal system. As an adult, Wade was ready to become violent at the drop of a hat. This physiological tendency went hand in hand with his being psychologically attuned to experience the world around him as violent.

How did Wade's family of origin, as internalized by Wade, shape the ways he responds to stress and assumes his responsibilities as a middle-aged man, father, adult son, and husband-to-be? From the descriptions of this alcoholic family's violence, neglect, and isolation, it is clear that Wade carried the cycle of violence into his own generation, unlike his brother Rolfe, who didn't fight back, didn't drink, and left to become a different kind of man, educated (a professor of history) and sensitive to the potential legacy of violence that he too had inherited.

At this point in his assessment of Wade's violence, the minister and the psychologist working with Wade need to consider Wade's relationship with Margie. Initially, Wade's relationship with Margie was a support to him. Margie's kindness, her easy way of relating, and her common sense calmed Wade down. She respected him and saw his struggles as normal, which was initially reassuring to him. Wade intuitively sensed that Margie was good for him and that her goodness would support his attempts to build a new family.

The minister and the psychologist noted that Wade and Margie's relationship, with its emerging intimacy, while fragile, did incorporate aspects of friendship and companionship. Margie's easy manner was part of her response to relational conflict. She did not experience a heightened physiological stress response to conflicts with Wade. It is important to note, however, that their intimacy had not yet weathered the seas of open conflict.

Margie was initially blind to the severity of the violence in the Whitehouse family. She hoped that Wade had not become like his father, but these hopes were being dispelled as Margie watched what happened when Glenn and Wade were together. She noticed similar mannerisms: gulping from beer or whiskey bottles that always seemed to be at hand, shaking salt on their fists and licking it off. She was shocked to glimpse the mutual hatred. When Margie was left in charge of Wade's father at the farmhouse, she was able to imagine what life was like for Wade's mother. Fortunately she did not identify with this role of the silent, suffering wife and was not inclined, as victims of past family violence and alcoholism often are, to accept the familiarity of violence and alcoholism. Instead, she realized the danger she was in and left the farmhouse, taking Jill with her. Unfortunately, she could not anticipate the level of violence that immediately erupted between Glenn and Wade as a result of her departure, violence that left Glenn dead and the farmhouse on fire.

Assessing Alcoholism

In a conversation subsequent to the one described in the verbatim, the minister asked Wade a series of questions about his use of alcohol (see chapter 6): how much he drank every day, what time he had his first drink, whether he ever felt uncomfortable when he couldn't get hold of a drink, whether he felt guilty about his drinking, whether he was annoyed when he was asked about his drinking (like right now), whether there were mornings when he couldn't remember what had happened the night before, and whether he ever regretted something he had said or done when he was drinking. Wade's responses led the minister to gain his permission to talk with his psychologist about his drinking. In addition to the questions asked by the minister, the psychologist asked Wade whether his siblings, parents, uncles, aunts, and grandparents abused alcohol or were alcoholics. Hearing that Wade's two older brothers who had been killed had abused alcohol and that his father was an alcoholic, the psychologist concluded that Wade was likely genetically predisposed to alcohol abuse and addiction. The psychologist also determined that Wade had used alcohol from adolescence to cope with stress.

Assessing Social Identity

Working together in caring for Wade, the minister and psychologist can further assess the effects of Wade's social identity upon his crisis. The culture of Lawford included the people who ran businesses in the town, those who were employed by these business, professionals who worked in educational and health organizations, and the large seasonal population present during the skiing, hunting, and summer recreational seasons. The basic culture of the town was New England individualism, where privacy is valued.

In assessing aspects of Wade's social identity, the minister can ask, Does Wade's social identity as a working-class, New England, middle-aged man help or hinder him in the crises he experiences? Wade has limited gender and class roles available to him. The town council gave him the job of parttime sheriff, but this job consisted mostly of directing traffic and issuing driving violations. Wade has worked for LaRivere's garage and snowplowing business since he graduated from high school. If LaRivere would not hire him back, who would? The patronage of the town council was not part of an interconnected support system in which everyone had dignity and could trust in a support system, no matter what happened. While Wade seemed oblivious to these dire circumstances, he likely experienced deep self-judgment, existential fears, and anxieties that drove his frenzied attempts to set up his new household.

The New England cultural values of individualism and privacy shape how the people in Lawford respond to Wade's alcoholism and violence. The minister assessing the response of townspeople to Glenn's or Wade's past alcoholism and violence sees these New England values represented in the way that alcoholism and violence were ignored and Glenn's wife and children were left to cope on their own. The religious communities of Lawford reflected and incorporated these same values.

Assessing particular aspects of Wade's social identity that are salient to his crisis, the minister should begin with gender and social class. Being male is a disadvantage for Wade because of the limited gender roles available to him in his family and community, especially because he lacked education and a profession. Although the town council offered him the job of parttime sheriff, his work identity was undermined by his duties on the snowplow and as traffic warden. He has internalized many of his culture's negative images of how tough men cope with stress by abusing alcohol, expressing anger but not feelings associated with emotional vulnerability, and becoming violent, and these images keep him trapped in dead-end jobs.

The most salient aspect of social identity for Wade, in his current crisis and throughout his life, is his social class and financial status. He struggled as a youth and adult to find work that would provide financial security and give him an identity or role that people in the town respected. Initially, when he married Lillian, he worked several jobs to try to achieve financial security, but the stress of this work life and his relational difficulties overwhelmed him. Throughout his life, his efforts to work hard and do a good job have been disrupted by his feelings, especially anger, by his alcoholism, and by his violence. While Alcoholics Anonymous was the most likely form of help available, he never availed himself of this resource, and there seem to have been no other resources, like effective pastoral care or psychological counseling, available to him. No one in his family or community has realized Wade's need for psychological assessment and intervention except his brother Rolfe, and then only in hindsight.

In terms of his age identity, Wade experiences both advantages and disadvantages having to do with his being at the midpoint of his life. The fact that he is aging was evident by his rotten tooth. Here the effects of age identity intertwine with class identity, for Wade seems not to have the resources or know-how to look after himself physically— not a good sign when one is middle-aged and looking ahead to possible increases in health problems. At the same time, his age is an advantage, if his own limitations and the limitations of his social identity do not overwhelm him and if he receives sufficient pastoral and psychological care, to start over again, build a new family, and find new work.

While Wade's sexual identity as a straight male appears not to be a salient issue at this point in his life, heterosexism has played a role in his formation. His father's insults to his sons always were about whether they were men or "candy-asses," that is, sissies. These insults seemed to form Wade's narrow views of what it means to be a man. At the beginning of his relationship with Lillian, he had the potential to become a sensitive man, more like his brother Rolfe. However, alcohol and violence replaced sensitivity when the stress of being married became too much.

This assessment of Wade's social identity can help the minister and psychologist understand what Wade experiences as a working-class man in a small New Hampshire town. His gender and social class work against him, in that he is caught in patterns that do not help him find ways to cope with his losses, violence, and alcoholism.

Theological Reflection

As the minister and psychologist assess what is going on psychologically for Wade, and understand how his gender and social class exacerbate his crisis, the minister can also theologically assess Wade's crisis. This assessment involves using the insights gained through the psychological assessment of the symbolic role played by his younger co-worker Jack and also the role played by the new family Wade envisioned. These symbols can be explored theologically, using Neville's perspectives described in chapter 7.

The minister can begin this assessment by considering the psychologist's conclusion that Wade experienced Jack as a symbol of the younger version of himself. Wade claims, "I know that kid, I know what he's like inside. He's a lot like I was when I was his age" (Banks 1989, 172). Another important symbol for Wade is the new family that he fervently wants to create. These two symbols—Jack as a younger version of himself and the redeemed family—have not only psychological meaning, but also theological meaning, in that they concern what Neville calls the boundary conditions of his crisis. Wade feels energized by an almost manic urgency to confront Jack, a symbol of his younger self, and create a family with Margie, Jill, and his father, a symbol of the redeemed family. The life-and-death quality of these two symbols is what gives them psychological and theological significance. For this reason, his symbols can be treated as religious and interpreted using Neville's theology.

Interpreting Symbols

The role of the pastoral caregiver is to help Wade interpret his symbols, initially by helping Wade cope with the intense urgency that makes him act impulsively. The reflective space in which to do such interpretation could be created after issues of safety have been addressed, as will be noted later in the chapter, in the discussion of a plan of care.

After identifying the symbols of Jack and the ideal family, the minister can assess whether Wade is able to interpret them. One way to answer this question is to explore Wade's experience of himself as stupid, an experience to which he alluded when he talked about the tender intimacy he first experienced with Lillian. Wade contrasted his frequent experience of feeling stupid with his potential for intelligence, which he glimpsed in his relationship with Lillian:

> [H]e had looked in [Lillian's] eyes way back then, when they were both high school kids, and he had seen her intelligence, the wonderful complexity of her awareness, and he had seen his own smart eyes looking back at him, and for a while he had felt intelligent too.
>
> (Banks 1989, 321)

Wade's brother Rolfe describes Wade's declining experiences of intelligence this way: "All those solitary dumb angry men, Wade and Pop and his father and grandfather, had once been boys with intelligent eyes and brightly innocent mouths, unafraid and loving creatures eager to please and be pleased" (Banks 1989, 322).

The tragedy of Wade's life is that this intelligence has been beaten out of him. His ways of coping, including violence and alcoholism, have resulted from chronic neglect and abuse and make it nearly impossible for Wade to regain that intelligence. Wade is acutely aware of his "stupidity":

> He had tried, Lord, how he had tried to break through the pain and confusion of his life to something like clarity and control, and it had come to this—this dumb helplessness, this woeful thickened shameful inadequacy. At bottom, he knew, there was love in his

heart—love for Jill that was as coherent and pure as algebra, and maybe even love for Margie too, and love for Ma, poor Ma, who was dead now and gone from him forever, and love for Lillian, in spite of everything: love for *women*—but try as he might he could not arrange his life so that he could act on that love. There were other things that kept getting in the way, his rage and his fear and his feelings of pure distress.

(Banks 1989, 320)

In this statement Wade acknowledges for the first time grief for his mother. He acknowledges that he doesn't know how to express his deep love for any of the women in his life. The minister can listen with empathy and underscore the importance of Wade's statement. He can also explore with Wade whether God is revealed in a love as "coherent and pure as algebra."

Various opportunities, like Wade's declaration of his love and helplessness, present themselves for Wade to engage in such interpretation. Seeing Jack as a younger version of himself presents an opportunity to talk about his past with Margie, Rolfe, his minister, and his psychologist, all of whom can help him interpret his embedded beliefs system and practices. Such a conversation between Wade and Margie does begin one evening when they are particularly close to each other. Wade talks with Margie about his similarity with Jack, but he ends up focusing on Jack and the hunting accident, rather than himself.

Wade also has the opportunity to understand his past in new ways when he and Rolfe are together after the funeral of their mother. Rolfe attempts to explore the violence Wade experienced as a child, but Wade brushes off his questions with a bewildered look that is followed by a guffaw of laughter and a swig from his father's whiskey bottle. If, in this conversation, Wade were able to remember how painful his childhood was, he would feel the full sadness and injustice of suffering, and he might experience a revelation of God's presence with those who suffer. His confusion and "stupidity" would dissipate, and he might be able to reexperience a love that is "as coherent and pure as algebra."

Assessing the Consequences of Wade's Symbols

The minister can next explore with Wade the consequences of his symbols. He can determine whether Wade realizes that he has acted impulsively, using the symbols of Jack as a younger version of himself, and

Margie and Jill as the ingredients for the redeemed family, concretely in ways that have been terribly destructive. He, for example, acted upon sudden aggressive impulses toward Jack, pursuing Jack's car in his boss's truck, and staging a violent life-threatening confrontation. He also treats Margie as an object, the wife/daughter-in-law/stepmother whom he can install in the farmhouse as though he is a puppeteer manipulating the next scene in the Whitehouse family play. He doesn't consider the consequences of his actions, doesn't ever see Jack as a person in his own right, doesn't wonder whether Margie can endure his father's hatred, violence, and alcoholism. Nor does he consider the consequences of bringing his daughter into this scenario. The actual consequence is a conflagration of violence, from which Margie barely escapes with Jill, and which leaves Glenn and Jack dead.

Assessing the State of Wade's Soul

The minister can next use Neville's theology to assess the state of Wade's soul. Banks poignantly describes Wade's teenaged soul, as "that lovely young thing, the fragile humorous affection for the world that he had nurtured and kept alive all through adolescence" (Banks 1989, 302). Wade tried to nurture his soul in the midst of his violent, alcoholic, and poverty-stricken home, and his intimate relationship with Lillian became a haven for his soul. This haven was destroyed by the violence and alcoholism which he used to cope with the stress of the adult responsibilities he assumed at an early age. He is not spiritually able to mourn these losses because he no longer has the intimate relationship with Lillian in which his complicated feelings can be expressed and understood. While his midlife crisis, evident in his intense interest in Jack and his dreams of redeeming his family, has reawakened his longing for a sense of soul, Wade does not have a deliberative belief system that allows him to work through earlier losses such that he can accept these losses and his limitations, and experience the presence of God in the very deepest part of himself. He does not have access to rich religious symbols, circles of friends, and a community that can help him make spiritual sense of his experiences.

His brother Rolfe speaks as a theologian when he describes a body without the soul as "a mere fact, a pile of minerals, a bag of waters" (Banks 1989, 340), using the following metaphor to describe the soul as relational:

If one regards the soul of the body as blood red membrane, let us say, a curling helix of anxiously fragile tissue that connects all the disparate nameable parts of the body to one another, a scarlet firmament between the firmaments, touching and defining both, one might view the soul of Wade's or any other life as that part of it which is connected to other lives. And one might grow angry and be struck with grief at the sight of those connections being severed, of that membrane being torn, shredded, rent to rags that a child grows into adulthood clinging to—little bloody flags waved vainly across a vast chasm.

(Banks 1989, 340)

Using Neville's theology of broken symbols, the minister concludes that Wade is not able to interpret his symbols of Jack as his younger self, and Margie and Jill as the ingredients of the redeemed family which he can single-handedly form. The minister can then turn to Poling's description of evil for further theological assessment.

Wade's Symbol System as Part of a Web of Violence, Not Life

The minister has uncovered the web of violence in which Wade, along with his father, has been caught. The term "affliction" describes the intergenerational cycle of raising boys who become men who use alcohol and violence to cope with life: "Boys who were beaten by their fathers, whose capacity for love and trust was crippled almost at birth and whose best hope for a connection to other human beings lay in elaborating for themselves an elegiac mode of relatedness, as if everyone's life were already over" (Banks 1986, 340). Banks begins the novel with a quote by Simone Weil: "The great enigma of human life is not suffering but affliction." Instead of being places of sacredness, family relationships are desecrated, becoming places where violence is reenacted.[2]

Wade's brother Rolfe realizes that he is also afflicted with this legacy of violence and alcoholism. He chooses to remain single, and not enter a committed, intimate relationship, because remaining single is "how we keep from destroying in our turn our own children and terrorizing the women who have the misfortune to love us; it is how we absent ourselves from the tradition of male violence; it is how we decline the seductive role of avenging angel: we grimly accept the restraints of nothingness—of disconnection, isolation and exile" (Banks 1989, 340).

---

2. The term "desecration" has been used to describe victims' experiences (Doehring 1993b).

The word "demonic" is another theological term that the minister can use in convincing Wade of the terrible power of his symbols of Jack as a younger version of himself, and Margie and Jill as his ideal family. Using the theological terms "evil" and "demonic," the minister can talk with Wade about the finitude of the human condition, evidenced in the fragile intimacy which he and Lillian briefly shared. Reflecting on his father's violence and Wade's violence as a young man, he can confront Wade with the potential within human beings to do immense harm when they participate in webs of violence, not webs based on promises to remain faithful in covenanted relationships. Then he can explore with Wade the hope that Wade can change his life by (1) ending his drinking and violence, (2) mourning the losses he experienced as a young adult and in the process letting go of his obsession with Jack and the ideal family he wants to create, and (3) regaining his earlier experiences of intimacy in his relationship with Margie. If Wade can attain these goals, he can participate in a web of life, not violence.

Making Faith Claims

Combining Neville's theology of broken symbols with Poling's theology of evil, resistance, and the multivalency and ambiguity of God provides the minister with a multifaceted theological understanding of how Wade is caught in cycles of violence and addiction. The two norms derived from these perspectives (practicing goodness and using symbols in transformative ways) can become a basis for a plan of care and justice. The minister can help Wade, his family, and his community learn to use symbols to experience transcendent and incarnate mysteries in such a way that symbols can transform them all. This transformation is possible only when the cycle of violence and the symbols that maintain it are broken.

Plan of Care

The pastoral caregiver must take steps to help Wade end his abusive behavior. A minister trained to recognize Wade's violence as both a sin and a crime will develop a plan of care for helping Wade stop his alcoholic, violent actions, which put members of his family at lethal risk.[3]

---

3. For further writings on pastoral care with offenders, see Cooper-White (1995) and Poling (2003).

This plan incorporates the steps I have earlier identified: (1) attending to the careseeker's safety and building trust, (2) mourning losses, and (3) reconnecting with the goodness of life.

Step 1: Attending to Safety and Building Trust

The goal of the first step of this overall plan of care and justice is to protect those in danger by attending to safety and building trust. When Wade, his minister, and his psychologist coconstruct life-sustaining habits concerning violence and alcoholism that can be maintained, then safety can be established. Ensuring safety requires that caregivers consult with denominational representatives and local social services. It is likely that they will determine that Glenn needs to receive medical treatment for alcoholism and is not safe living in the farmhouse by himself or with Wade. With Wade's permission, the minister can have ongoing consultation with the health professionals who care for his father and determine his future needs.

The minister also can ask Margie privately if Wade has ever become physically violent with her. When he ascertains that this has not happened, he can review with her a plan should Wade become violent.

In ongoing conversations with Wade, he can continue to express his concern about how Wade expresses his anger and feelings of helplessness and refer him to a psychologist, who may refer Wade to a group for men who have been physically violent in intimate relationships. He can inquire closely about how Wade cares for Jill when she visits, reviewing with Wade how he handles intense feelings and whether there is ever a risk of him neglecting Jill or becoming physically violent.

The minister must recognize that to enact a program of "zero tolerance" of violence, he needs the help of law enforcement and judicial organizations that can intervene when violence occurs. He may find it difficult to change the way law enforcement and judicial bodies respond to violence. Working with law enforcement and judicial procedures for handling family violence, however, is a central task for pastoral caregivers or religious bodies at higher organizational levels. The enormous task of working to transform organizations that perpetuate violence is part of the first step of a plan seeking healing and justice.

If the minister is able to work with other professionals in Lawford to ensure the appropriate response to violence, Wade may be questioned by the police about his threatening behaviors, such as pushing his father up against the wall and tailgating and threatening Jack. The sooner he is held accountable for his violent behavior, the better. Being arrested and charged with assault is an important aspect of intervention, because until that happens, Wade may think that violence is a private matter within his family, and between him and Jack, and not a crime.

Another aspect of attending to safety involves Wade's great difficulty controlling his impulses and acting intentionally when he is drinking alcohol excessively. The minister can initially help Wade realize the extent of his problems with alcohol and refer him for treatment. Wade may not be sufficiently motivated to seek treatment until he has "hit bottom" in what is often a series of alcohol-related crises that get worse and worse. A well-timed intervention by the minister, Margie, and his co-workers may prompt him to seek help. The enormous challenge is for Wade to give up alcohol, because alcohol can, at least in the first several drinks, "serve as the nectar of hope, the elixir of anxiety and depression, . . . and may offer an alternative salvation from feeling disabled by despair" (Martignetti 2000).[4] An addiction counselor working with Wade can help him describe his "love" of alcohol and the losses of giving it up. He can begin attending 12-step groups like Alcoholic Anonymous, a kind of care that is accessible to a working-class man like Wade. A physician can assess whether Wade is so dependent that withdrawal will necessitate hospitalization. Wade is most likely to resist such treatment and is more likely to try abstinence. With enough motivation, he may succeed at it.[5] Such abstinence will not address the addiction or abuse, however, if Wade is simply depriving himself of one way to cope, and not coming to terms with the losses incurred throughout his life from the time he started to abuse alcohol. Just as Wade will need to confront the losses associated with violence and empathize with those he hurt, so too will he need to take "moral inventory" of the losses and harm incurred by drinking (one of the twelve steps in Alcoholics Anonymous and part of a long-term repentance process).

This first part of this plan of care addresses the roles of the culture, the community, and a team of caregivers in dealing with the violence and alcoholism that form the habits of Wade's daily life, as well as the habits of many of the working-class men who live in his town. These

---

4. Martignetti (2000) goes on to describe how alcohol "steals pain and soothes loneliness . . . is the creator of possibility, the deity upon which rests eternal dreams, . . . is the currency of connection to others, filling the void left by a lack of intimacy."

5. Members and counselors using Alcoholics Anonymous and many mental health professionals see abstinence as the only long-term solution to alcoholism. They believe that once an abstainer takes one drink, he or she will not be able to control their drinking. Other addiction theorists and counselors who use cognitive behavioral theory and techniques say that people in recovery can eventually control their drinking. It may be that the severity and duration of the abuse/dependence may determine whether control or abstinence works (*Harvard Mental Health Letter*, June 2000, 3).

habits arise out of operational theologies that have their own symbols. In some cases a harsh, judgmental theology may be associated with sobriety and an idealistic, sentimental theology with being intoxicated. The alcoholic habits that underlie such theologies must be changed first, in order for operational theologies and their related symbols to become explicit and to change.

Not only Wade's habits and his operational theology, but also those of his family and community must change, so that violence and drinking will no longer be ignored. Wade's family can be involved in his plan of care (Clinebell 1998). Wade can meet with his brother and sister, perhaps with the pastoral caregiver, to talk about what it was like growing up in their family. In this arena, losses can be acknowledged. Family meetings may have a beneficial effect for Wade's siblings, perhaps prompting them to seek help for themselves. As well, the remnant of this family may be able to support each other in new ways and together plan the care of their father.

Step 2: Mourning Losses

The second step of caring for those caught in violence and addiction involves mourning the losses incurred by abuse and alcoholism. If Wade can break his habitual use of violence and alcohol to cope with intense longings and helplessness, he will, for the first time in his adult life, face the full impact of the losses he has incurred throughout his whole life. He has been unable fully to experience them because violence has kept him from fully processing the losses, and alcohol has numbed him to them. At this step in care, the caregiver can begin addressing the losses that Wade is acutely and unconsciously experiencing in his midlife crisis. The caregiver can begin by discussing with Wade his feelings about Jack and what it was like for Wade when he was Jack's age.

Wade will experience intense grief as he faces the many unacknowledged losses that have been part of his life. He experienced the loss of a safe, secure childhood. He may now be able also to experience the losses and suffering of his mother and siblings at the hands of his father, as well as his father's own deprivation in childhood. He may also fully experience the losses he incurred by entering adult life too soon. The psychologist can work with Wade to understand his obsession with Jack and the new family he wants to create, because now Wade is more able to stop using these symbols in concrete, unconscious ways. Wade may now be able to interpret such symbols and begin constructing new symbols, based upon his new behavior of not being violent and not drinking. Repentance, the long process of coming to terms with destructive behavior, depends upon his ability to construct new symbols associated with transcendence as he struggles to come to terms with losses. This process of repentance is best done in the context of a faith community whose life arises out of the kind of religious symbols that Wade uses to make sense of his suffering.

Wade's minister, working with his psychologist, can offer help in this step of mourning losses. He can bring the rich symbols of mourning that are part of all religious traditions. The stories of the exodus in Hebrew Scripture, the intense feelings expressed in the psalms, the lamentations of the prophets, the stories about suffering, crucifixion, and resurrection in the Gospels and the book of Acts, as well as the testimonies of the leaders of early Christian communities, offer many ways of understanding loss, violence, and redemption. The minister can also help Wade experience a sense of grace. As Mercadante (1996) observed, grace is part of a restored covenant with God in which God takes the initiative, touching people when they hit bottom, or immediately after a trigger event, when they are at risk of breaking the covenant again. The religious practices based upon a belief in God's grace may be resources that, along with psychotherapeutic and psychopharmacological care, can sustain Wade as he mourns his losses and faces the losses of his victims.

Step 3: Reconnecting with the Ordinariness of Life

The final step, which may begin concurrently with step 2, is to reconnect with ordinary life. The psychologist can identify the new skills Wade may need as he reconnects and can guide him toward ways to enhance his social skills. Since his job opportunities may be limited in Lawford, acquiring more or different job skills may be part of a long-term plan. Of special concern is the type of work environment Wade will be in, since his historic work environments have not supported developing good communication skills, coping well with stress, and avoiding alcohol and violence. His reconnection with ordinary life can be sustained and enhanced if he participates in a faith community. For example, Wade can reexperience both his suffering and his new life in the light of the seasons of the church year.

As he reconnects with the ordinariness of human life, he may slowly be able to accept the ambiguities and complexity of a finite life, especially if he is part of relationships and faith communities that encourage such acceptance. In the midst of such relationships and communities, he may be able to construct more life-giving symbols that carry over values of an unconditioned infinite realm, such as are depicted in his lost Christian traditions. If he and others in relationship with him can use such symbols intentionally, they may be able to resist evil and practice goodness in ways that transform themselves and their families, communities, and cultures.

These steps may represent a lifelong plan for Wade, but this plan can easily be blocked at any step. As can be readily seen, care of this nature cannot be provided solely by a pastoral caregiver. A team of caregivers and a supportive faith community need to effect such care and justice. Pastoral caregivers, in a team setting, can have an enormous impact if they can help to attend to safety for victims and bring about changes in law enforcement and judicial processes such that an effective intervention can be made to help Wade end his violent behavior. While this may not be possible in Wade's community, nonetheless, transforming community systems must remain an ideal for pastoral caregivers. Working closely with health professionals, the minister can play a pivotal role in helping Wade find life-giving ways of coping that are not violent or addictive. He can also help him mourn his losses with rich religious symbols and in communities that can help him act intentionally on these symbols and ultimately reconnect with life.

For all people of faith, recovery must become a way of life, because those who have renounced addictive ways of coping are always vulnerable to reverting to such coping when stress is intense, and when families, communities, and cultures do not support them. In some ways, the challenges faced by those in recovery are the same challenges that all peoples of religious faith face: living out one's deepest faith commitments and beliefs in the complex webs of relational needs that are part of life in many contexts today. Faith-based relationships (with God, with those with whom we live and work, within communities of faith) ought to form a web of promises that can sustain those who seek healing and justice for themselves, their brothers and sisters, and all creation.

Conclusion

In the twenty-first century, pastoral caregivers face the challenge of how to offer care that draws upon contemporary postmodern approaches to knowledge, as well as centuries-old premodern and modern religious traditions of Christianity. I offer the metaphor of trifocal lenses to suggest ways in which pastoral caregivers can use (1) premodern norms of interpreting religious sources of authority in order to focus on the careseeker's connection with the sacred, (2) modern norms utilized in biblical critical methods, the social sciences, and medical studies to develop broad or general ways of understanding the careseeker's suffering, and (3) postmodern norms utilized in cultural and theological studies to understand the careseeker's social identity and possible experiences of social oppression, and to coconstruct provisional meanings, especially theological norms, upon which care can be based.

In this conclusion, I articulate more fully how the kind of care described in this book can be described as postmodern because of its narrative, contextual, cross-disciplinary, and pragmatic aspects. I draw upon Scalise's (2003) recent descriptions of narrative, contextual, and correlational approaches to practical theology in order to locate my approach within ongoing discussions of methodology in pastoral theology.

Narrative Pastoral Theology

My approach to pastoral care begins with pastoral care conversations and the careseeker's narratives about self, family, community, and culture. For many people this is a comfortable and safe way to begin a conversation about their difficulties, since people tend to organize their descriptions of what is happening to them in narratives that "reflect the story-like character of much human experience" (Scalise 2003, 107).

Focusing on the particularity of stories is a hallmark of a postmodern approach (Lartey 2003). When caregivers immerse themselves in the details of the narratives that unfold in pastoral care, they are less likely to miss narrative complexities and ambiguities that are lost when caregivers move too quickly to using diagnostic categories. This immersion in the story allows caregivers "to find an important place for parts of human experience and data like emotions, the symbolic and the irrational, . . . [parts necessary] to fully address the human condition" (Pattison and Woodward 2000, 13). Caregivers who listen to careseekers' stories as if they were artistic renderings of life will apprehend the mystical and aesthetic experience of these stories, and not just the moral experience that is highlighted when they use an ethical approach (Sands 1994).

There are of course several liabilities in using only a narrative approach. First, in an individualistic culture, caregivers may focus so exclusively on the person of the careseeker that cultural contexts are a blurred background.[1] This critique has been made in reference to both narrative theologies and constructivist psychology, because they focus exclusively on how individuals construct narratives about who they are. The ways in which careseekers are formed by their cultural contexts and the role of social privilege or disadvantage in their crises are left out of the picture.

Second, in using narrative pastoral theology, the caregiver runs the risk of becoming immersed in the aesthetic and mystical aspects of the careseeker's narrative, making it difficult to focus on its moral aspects. Much like postmodern literary theorists adept at exploring the multi-

---

1. In the 1960s and '70s, pastoral caregivers used a therapeutic paradigm (Patton 1993) in which care was enacted in one-on-one psychotherapeutic relationships. In this individualistic clinical mode, the goal of treatment was individual psychological change. When pastoral caregivers used systems perspectives, they saw the internestedness of the biological and intrapsychic systems of the individual in family, community, and cultural systems. When the influence of the cultural system for those experiencing social oppression was taken into account, practitioners appreciated that individual and familial transformation was not possible without social transformation.

ple meanings of a text, caregivers using a narrative approach may resist (1) making judgments about the moral dimensions of a careseeker's story and (2) positing provisional faith claims that can become the basis for a plan of care. Scalise (2003, 108) attributes this resistance to "the gap between the narrative world and the everyday world of moral action and struggle."

Contextual Pastoral Theology

When caregivers relate the careseeker's story to the "metanarratives" (Lyotard 1984) of the culture, their care becomes contextual. Metanarratives are a culture's underlying values and myths, for example, the myth of scientific progress—that modern Western culture is progressing in a direction in which scientific knowledge will accumulate until problems that cause suffering are solved. This belief in scientific progress may provide hope when careseekers focus on physical aspects of suffering and wish for medication to dull the pain or halt the spread of cancer. But science often can't provide remedies for spiritual and emotional pain. Soldiers wounded in battle may receive the best available medical attention in the aftermath of combat and still carry deep psychic wounds. Another metanarrative in the United States is belief in the power of the individual to conquer all odds and rise to success—the self-made man or woman, often portrayed in the media. The role of metanarratives like a belief in science and individual success in shaping peoples' worldviews, their beliefs, and their construction of knowledge is highlighted when caregivers use a contextual approach. Attending to cultural metanarratives and their political dimensions is a feature of a postmodern approach to knowledge.

In another way a contextual approach reflects postmodern approaches to knowledge: caregivers can think about their social location and how their attitudes are shaped by metanarratives that may blind them to certain aspects of suffering. The pastoral caregiver who is able to gain a perspective on her social privileges and their accompanying assumptions is "decentered" and "encounters in the other (person, culture, religion) irreducible difference that is no longer subject to standards of the implicit or explicit values of the worldview in which the observing self stands. The inevitable linkage of knowledge and power is now acknowledged" (Ramsay 2004, 6). A caregiver who draws upon this "critical sensibility" (Ramsay 2004, 6) recognizes in herself a quickness to judge those who may not share her ability to be articulate and lucid—abilities gained through educational opportunities.

Self-reflexivity—critically reflecting on one's assumptions and social privilege—is an important part of providing care that avoids contributing to social oppression and injustice. While being accountable for the very assumptions of knowledge that are used is a tall order, caregivers must work toward this ideal by being in dialogue with those from different cultures concerning the cultural relevance and possible colonialist implications of their approaches to pastoral care.

Cross-Disciplinary Pastoral Theology

The need for interdisciplinary dialogue is especially important in a postmodern approach to caregiving, in which no single disciplinary perspective yields transhistorical universal truths about a careseeker's suffering. When careseekers assume that the knowledge of any disciplinary perspective is socially constructed, they are able to listen for the ways in which one perspective may help them critique another. For example, many modern psychological models of personality and therapeutic approaches are based upon implicit ethical and religious assumptions. Pastoral theologian Don Browning utilizes a hermeneutical method to identify these assumptions and beliefs in the theories of Freud, humanistic psychology, Skinner, Jung, Erikson, Kohut, Ellis, Beck, and Bowen (Browning and Cooper 2004). He illustrates how these modern psychologies are "mixed disciplines that contain examples of religious, ethical, and scientific language" (Browning and Cooper 2004, 7); having uncovered the "full normative horizon" of these psychologies, he critically evaluates them (Browning and Cooper 2004, 18).

Besides listening for ways in which disciplinary perspectives may be at odds with each other, careseekers can also listen for the ways in which they illuminate different aspects of suffering such that a deeper, more complex understanding is formed. Such congruence can be provisionally understood as a confirmation that each discipline is relevant and meaningful, the hallmarks of perspectival truth in a postmodern approach to knowledge.

A cross-disciplinary approach that values both the consonance and dissonance between disciplinary perspectives has to do more with correlation and less with integration. Psychologists of religion committed to integration look for "the discovery and articulation of the common underlying principles" of psychology and theology (Eck 1996, 102) that result in "a greater, more holistic and unified understanding of human persons and their social/ecosystemic worlds" (Eck 1996, 102). The danger of integrating disciplinary perspectives is that one perspective, often theology for postliberal pastoral caregivers and explicitly Christian psychologists of religion, becomes subsumed under psychology and the social sciences. This "unification" approach is a liability when it results in rigid norms being used to interpret religious sources of authority in a way that renders singular meanings. Such rigidity can be experienced across a theological spectrum, from conserving to reconstructing theologies. Rigidity shuts down the creative process of generating multiple paradoxical meanings (like the tension between despair and hope that is part of a lament). A critical correlational approach to cross-disciplinary perspectives on suffering is congruent with a postmodern appreciation for multiplicity and ambiguity.

Pragmatic Pastoral Theology

While scholars who use postmodern approaches to knowledge often engage in abstract reflections, practitioners who use such approaches must attempt to articulate provisional knowledge claims that can become a basis for action. Given their distinctive use of theological perspectives, pastoral practitioners articulate their knowledge claims in theological terminology. Such statements are difficult to formulate because each theological perspective involves specialized terminology and complex theories. The difference between understanding various theological perspectives and formulating knowledge claims can be described as the difference between theological literacy and fluency (Doehring 2002). Practitioners of the pastoral arts of ministry attempt to move from literacy to fluency, for example, in preparing sermons that bring biblical exegesis into conversation with an exegesis of culture and congregation; Paul Tillich demonstrated fluency by being able to preach sermons whose basic knowledge claims resonated with his systematic theology. The irony of theological education is that the more specialized, or literate, teachers and students become, the more difficult it can be to become fluent in using these perspectives as practitioners.

Using a postmodern approach to knowledge, practitioners of pastoral care make provisional, but not arbitrary claims: the claims are based on disciplinary perspectives and also a cross-disciplinary under-standing of suffering that, because it is explicit, can be assessed by scholars and practitioners from various specializations. Contextual claims need not be limited to the situations in which they arise; they may be relevant in a variety of similar situations. These provisional theological claims become the basis for liberating praxis in which provisional truth claims are affirmed through action.[2]

Having described the need for pastoral care based on postmodern approaches to knowledge to be narrative, contextual, cross-disciplinary, and pragmatic, in the final analysis, I want to acknowledge a basic post-modern assumption: that there are no universal, transhistorical definitions of pastoral care. The description of pastoral care I articulate is, in the end, a local tradition of care that arises out of my scholarly and pastoral practices. What is needed at this point in the history of pastoral care is the articulation of local traditions, and conversations among these traditions, so that we can learn from each other.

---

2. "Truth can only be known or affirmed through action, and therefore the ability of feminist [or, for that matter, any] theology to inspire and reflect liberating action in specific contexts is the criterion for judging its truth. Relativism and rampant individualism [are] avoided by emphasizing that the task of doing theology is a communal exercise" (Stuart and Thatcher 1997, 154–55).

References

Adams, Carol J. 1994. *Women Battering*. Minneapolis: Augsburg Fortress.

Adams, Jay E. 1970. *Competent to Counsel*. Phillipsburg, NJ: Presbyterian & Reformed.

Adams, Jay E. 1986. *How to Help People Change: The Four-Step Biblical Process*. Grand Rapids: Ministry Resources Library.

American Psychiatric Association. 2000. *Diagnostic and Statistical Manual of Mental Health Disorders*, 4th ed., text revised. Washington, DC: American Psychiatric Association.

Anderson, Herbert, and Robert Cotton Fite. 1994. *Becoming Married*. Louisville, KY: Westminster/John Knox.

Anderson, Herbert, and Kenneth R. Mitchell. 1993. *Leaving Home*. Louisville, KY: Westminster/John Knox.

Attig, Thomas. 2000. *The Heart of Grief: Death and the Search for Lasting Love*. New York: Oxford University Press.

Augsburger, D. W. 1986. *Pastoral Counseling Across Cultures*. Philadelphia: Westminster.

Banks, Russell. 1989. *Affliction*. San Francisco: HarperPerennial.

Boisen, Anton. 1936. *The Exploration of the Inner World: A Study of Mental Disorder and Religious Experience*. New York: Willett, Clark & Co. Reprints; New York: Harper & Brothers, 1952; Philadelphia: University of Pennsylvania Press, 1971.

Bonanno, G. A. 2004. Loss, Trauma, and Human Resilience: Have We Underestimated the Human Capacity to Thrive after Extremely Aversive Events? *American Psychologist* 59: 20–28.

Browning, Donald S. 1991. *A Fundamental Practical Theology: Descriptive and Strategic Proposals*. Minneapolis: Fortress.

Browning, Donald S., and Terry Cooper. 2004. *Religious Thought and Modern Psychologies,* 2nd ed. Minneapolis: Fortress.

Bullis, Ronald. 1990. When Confessional Walls Have Ears: The Changing Clergy Privileged Communications Law. *Pastoral Psychology* 39 (2): 75–84.

Carver, Raymond. 1988. A Small, Good Thing. In *Where I'm Calling From: New and Selected Stories*, 280–301. New York: Atlantic Monthly Press.

Clebsch, William A., and Charles R. Jaekle. 1964. *Pastoral Care in Historical Perspective: An Essay with Exhibits*. Englewood Cliffs, NJ: Prentice-Hall.

Clinebell, Howard. 1998. *Understanding and Counseling Persons with Alcohol, Drug, and Behavioral Addictions.* Nashville: Abingdon.

Cooper-White, Pamela. 1995. *The Cry of Tamar: Violence against Women and the Church's Response.* Minneapolis: Fortress.

Cooper-White, Pamela. 2003. *Shared Wisdom: Use of Self in Pastoral Care and Counseling.* Minneapolis: Fortress.

Couture, Pamela D. 2003. The Effect of Postmodernism on Pastoral/Practical Theology and Care and Counseling. *Journal of Pastoral Theology* 13 (Spring): 85–104.

Dann, Bucky. 2002. *Addiction Pastoral Responses.* Nashville: Abingdon.

Davaney, Sheila Greeve. 2000. *Pragmatic Historicism: A Theology for the Twenty-first Century.* Albany: State University of New York Press.

Denham, Thomas E., and Melinda Denham. 1986. Avoiding Malpractice Suits in Pastoral Counseling. *Pastoral Psychology* 35: 83–93.

Doehring, Carrie. 1987. The Darkness of Violence, the Light of God's Healing: An Advent Worship Liturgy. In Marie Fortune, ed., *Keeping the Faith: Questions and Answers for the Abused Woman,* 69–71. San Francisco: Harper & Row.

Doehring, Carrie. 1993a. The Absent God: When Neglect Follows Sexual Violence. *Journal of Pastoral Care* 47 (Summer): 3–12.

Doehring, Carrie. 1993b. *Internal Desecration: Traumatization and Representations of God.* Lanham, MD: University Press of America.

Doehring, Carrie. 1995. *Taking Care: Monitoring Power Dynamics and Relational Boundaries in Pastoral Care and Counseling.* Nashville: Abingdon.

Doehring, Carrie. 1999. A Method of Feminist Pastoral Theology. In B. Gill-Austern and B. Miller-McLemore, eds., *Feminist and Womanist Pastoral Theology,* 95–111. Nashville: Abingdon.

Doehring, Carrie. 2002. Theological Literacy and Fluency in a New Millennium: A Pastoral Theological Perspective. In Rodney L. Petersen with Nancy M. Rourke, eds., *Theological Literacy for the Twenty-first Century,* 311–24. Grand Rapids: Eerdmans.

Doka, K. J., ed. 1989. *Disenfranchised Grief: Recognizing Hidden Sorrow.* Lexington, MA: Lexington Books.

Doyle, Roddy. 1996. *The Woman Who Walked into Doors.* New York: Penguin.

Eck, Brian E. 1996. Integrating the Integrators: An Organizing Framework for a Multifaceted Process of Integration. *Journal of Psychology and Christianity* 15: 101–15.

Egan, Gerard. 1994. *The Skilled Helper: A Problem-Management Approach to Helping,* 5th ed. Pacific Grove, CA: Brooks/Cole.

Ekman, P. 1993. Facial Expression and Emotion. *American Psychologist* 48 (4): 384–92.

Erenberg, Debra, and George Hacker. 1997. Problem? What Problem? Some Basic Facts about the Drinking Culture. In *Last Call for High-Risk Bar Pro-*

motions That Target College Students: A Community Action Guide. (www.health .org/govpubs/rpo995).

Fortune, Marie M. 1983. *Sexual Violence: The Unmentionable Sin.* New York: Pilgrim.

Fortune, Marie M. 1987. *Keeping the Faith: Questions and Answers for the Abused Woman.* San Francisco: Harper & Row.

Fortune, Marie M. 1988. Reporting Child Abuse: An Ethical Mandate for Ministry. In Anne L. Horton and Judith A. Williamson, eds., *Abuse and Religion,* 189–97. Lexington, MA: Lexington Books.

Fortune, Marie M. 1989. *Is Nothing Sacred? When Sex Invades the Pastoral Relationship.* San Francisco: Harper & Row.

Fortune, Marie M., and James Poling. 1995. Calling to Accountability: The Church's Response to Abusers. In Carol J. Adams and Marie M. Fortune, eds., *Violence Against Women and Children: A Christian Theological Sourcebook,* 451–63. New York: Continuum.

Gergen, Kenneth J. 2001. Psychological Science in a Post-Modern Context. *American Psychologist* 56 (10): 803–13.

Gerkin, Charles V. 1986. *Widening the Horizons: Pastoral Response to a Fragmented Society.* Philadelphia: Westminster.

Gottman, John. 1999. *The Seven Principles for Making Marriage Work.* New York: Crown.

Graham, Larry Kent. 1992. *Care of Person, Care of World: A Psychosystems Approach to Pastoral Care and Counseling.* Nashville: Abingdon.

Graham, Larry Kent. 2004. Theodicy, Tragedy, and Literature. Unpublished lecture notes from a course, Theodicy and Tragedy. Denver, CO: Iliff School of Theology.

Hagman, George. 2002. Beyond Cathexis: Toward a New Psychoanalytic Understanding and Treatment of Mourning. In Robert A. Neimeyer, ed., *Meaning Reconstruction and the Experience of Loss,* 13–31. Washington, DC: American Psychological Association.

Harvard Mental Health Letter. 2000. Treatment of Alcoholism, Parts 1 and 2. Boston: Harvard Health Publications. May, June, 2000: 1–4.

Herman, Judith. 1992. *Trauma and Recovery: The Aftermath of Violence—from Domestic Abuse to Political Terror.* New York: Basic Books.

Hoff, Lee Ann. 1989. *People in Crisis: Understanding and Helping,* 3rd ed. Redwood City, CA: Addison-Wesley.

Imbens, Annie, and Ineke Jonker. 1992. *Christianity and Incest,* trans. Patricia McVay. Minneapolis: Fortress.

Karaban, Roslyn A. 1991. The Sharing of Cultural Variation. *Journal of Pastoral Care* 45: 25–34.

Karaban, Roslyn A. 2000. *Complicated Losses, Difficult Deaths: A Practical Guide for Ministering to Grievers.* San Jose, CA: Resource Publications.

Kidd, Sue Monk. 2002. *The Secret Lives of Bees.* New York: Viking.

Klass, Dennis. 2002. The Inner Representation of the Dead Child in the Psychic and Social Narratives of Bereaved Parents. In Robert A. Neimeyer, ed., *Meaning Reconstruction and the Experience of Loss*, 77–94. Washington, DC: American Psychological Association.

Kluckhohn, Clyde, and Henry A. Murray, eds. 1948. *Personality in Nature, Society and Culture*. New York: Knopf.

Lakeland, Paul. 1997. *Postmodernity: Christian Identity in a Fragmented Age*. Minneapolis: Fortress.

Lartey, Emmanuel Y. 2002. Embracing the Collage: Pastoral Theology in an Era of 'Post-Phenomena.' *Journal of Pastoral Theology* 12 (Fall): 1–10.

Lartey, Emmanuel Y. 2003. *In Living Color: An Intercultural Approach to Pastoral Care and Counseling*, 2nd ed. New York: Jessica Kingsley.

Lartey, Emmanuel Y. 2004. Globalization, Internationalization, and Indigenization of Pastoral Care and Counseling. In Nancy J. Ramsay, ed., *Pastoral Care and Counseling: Redefining the Paradigms*, 87–108. Nashville: Abingdon.

Linehan, Marsha. 1993. *Cognitive Behavioral Treatment of Borderline Personality Disorder*. New York: Guilford Press.

Lyall, Katherine. 1995. Binge Drinking in College: A Definitive Study in Binge Drinking on American College Campuses: A New Look at an Old Problem. A Report Supported by the Robert Wood Foundation.

Lyotard, Jean Francois. 1984. *The Postmodern Condition: A Report on Knowledge*, trans. Geoff Bennington and Brian Massumi. Theory and History of Literature, 10. Minneapolis: University of Minnesota Press.

Martignetti, Anthony. 2000. A Workshop on Pro-Symptom Approaches to the Treatment of Alcoholism. Unpublished manuscript. Lexington, MA.

McCarthy, Marie. 1992. Empathy: A Bridge Between. *Journal of Pastoral Care* 46: 119–28.

McGoldrick, Monica, Randy Gerson, and Sylvia Shellenberger. 1999. *Genograms: Assessment and Interventions*, 2nd ed. New York: W. W. Norton.

Mercadante, Linda A. 1996. *Victims and Sinners: Spiritual Roots of Addiction and Recovery*. Louisville, KY: Westminster John Knox.

Miller-McLemore, Bonnie. 1996. The Living Human Web: Pastoral Theology at the Turn of the Century. In Jeanne Stevenson Moessner, ed., *Through the Eyes of Women*, 9–26. Minneapolis: Fortress.

Mitchell, Kenneth R., and Herbert Anderson. 1983. *All Our Losses, All Our Griefs: Resources for Pastoral Care*. Philadelphia: Westminster.

Morgan, Oliver J., and Merle Jordan, eds. 1999. *Addiction and Spirituality: A Multidisciplinary Approach*. St. Louis: Chalice.

Morrison, Toni. 1987. *Beloved*. New York: Penguin.

Neimeyer, R. A. 1995. Constructivist Psychotherapies: Features, Foundations, and Future Directions. In R. A. Neimeyer and M. J. Mahoney, eds., *Constructivism in Psychotherapy*, 11–38. Washington, DC: American Psychological Association.

Neimeyer, R. A., and J. D. Raskin, eds. 2000. *Constructions of Disorders: Meaning Making Frameworks for Psychotherapy.* Washington, DC: American Psychological Association.

Neimeyer, R. A., ed. 2001. *Meaning Reconstruction and the Experience of Loss.* Washington, DC: American Psychological Association.

Nelson, James B. 2004. *Thirst: God and the Alcoholic Experience.* Louisville, KY: Westminster John Knox.

Neuger, Christie Cozad. 2001. *Counseling Women: A Narrative, Pastoral Approach.* Minneapolis: Fortress.

Neville, Robert. 1996. *The Truth of Broken Symbols.* New York: SUNY.

Okum, Barbara F., Jane Fried, and Marcia L. Okum. 1999. *Understanding Diversity: A Learning-as-Practice Primer.* Pacific Grove, CA: Brooks/Cole.

Pargament, Kenneth I. 1997. *The Psychology of Religion and Coping: Theory, Research, Practice.* New York: Guilford.

Pargament, Kenneth I., and Annette Mahoney. 2002. Spirituality: Discovering and Conserving the Sacred. In C. R. Snyder and S. J. Lopez, eds., *Handbook of Positive Psychology,* 646–59. New York: Oxford University Press.

Park, Andrew Sung. 1993. *The Wounded Heart of God.* New York: Maryknoll.

Park, Andrew Sung. 1996. *Racial Conflict and Healing.* New York: Maryknoll.

Pattison, Stephen. 1998. Suffer Little Children: The Challenge of Child Abuse and Neglect to Theology. *Journal of Sexuality and Theology* 9: 36–58.

Pattison, Stephen, and James Woodward. 2000. An Introduction to Pastoral and Practical Theology. In James Woodward and Stephen Pattison, eds., *The Blackwell Reader in Pastoral and Practical Theology,* 1–19. Oxford: Blackwell.

Patton, John. 1993. *Pastoral Care in Context: An Introduction to Pastoral Care.* Louisville, KY: Westminster/John Knox.

Pellauer, Mary, Barbara Chester, and Jane Boyajian, eds. 1987. *Sexual Assault and Abuse: A Handbook for Clergy and Religious Professionals.* San Francisco: Harper & Row.

Poling, James N. 1980. *A Theological Integration of the Personal and Social in Pastoral Care and Counseling.* PhD Diss., School of Theology, Claremont, CA.

Poling, James N. 1991. *The Abuse of Power: A Theological Problem.* Nashville: Abingdon.

Poling, James N. 1996. *Deliver Us from Evil: Resisting Racial and Gender Oppression.* Minneapolis: Fortress.

Poling, James N. 2003. *Understanding Male Violence: Pastoral Care Issues.* St. Louis: Chalice.

Poling, James N., and Donald E. Miller. 1985. *Foundations for a Practical Theology of Ministry.* Nashville: Abingdon.

Poortinga, Y. A., N. H. Shoots, and J. M. Van de Koppel. 1993. The Understanding of Chinese and Kurdish Emblematic Gestures by Dutch Subjects. *International Journal of Psychology* 28(1): 31–44.

Pretzell, P. W. 1990. Suicide (Ethical Issues); Suicide (Pastoral Care); Suicide

Prevention. In Rodney Hunter, ed., *Dictionary of Pastoral Care and Counseling,* 1233–35. Nashville: Abingdon.

Ramsay, Nancy J. 1991. Sexual Abuse and Shame: The Travail of Recovery. In Maxine Glaz and Jeanne S. Moessner, eds., *Women in Travail and Transition: A New Pastoral Care,* 109–25. Nashville: Abingdon.

Ramsay, Nancy J. 1998. *Pastoral Diagnosis: A Resource for Ministries of Care and Counseling.* Minneapolis: Fortress.

Ramsay, Nancy J. 2000. Truth, Power, and Love: Challenges for Clergywomen across the Life Span. In Jeanne Stevenson-Moessner, ed., *In Her Own Time: Women and Developmental Issues in Pastoral Care,* 269–83. Minneapolis: Fortress.

Ramsay, Nancy J. 2002. Navigating Racial Difference as a White Pastoral Theologian. *Journal of Pastoral Theology* 12 (Fall): 11–27.

Ramsay, Nancy J. 2004. A Time of Ferment and Redefinition. In Nancy Ramsay, ed., *Pastoral Care and Counseling: Redefining the Paradigms,* 1–64. Nashville: Abingdon.

Rediger, G. Lloyd. 2003. *Beyond the Scandals: A Guide for Healthy Sexuality for Clergy.* Minneapolis: Fortress.

Rizzuto, Ana-Maria. 1979. *Birth of the Living God: A Psychoanalytic Study.* Chicago: University of Chicago Press.

Rutter, Peter. 1989. *Sex in the Forbidden Zone: When Men in Power Abuse Women's Trust.* Los Angeles: Jeremy Tarcher.

Sands, Kathleen M. 1994. *Escape from Paradise: Evil and Tragedy in Feminist Theology.* Minneapolis: Fortress.

Savage, John. 1996. *Listening and Caring Skills: A Guide for Groups and Leaders.* Nashville: Abingdon.

Scalise, Charles. 2003. *Bridging the Gap.* Nashville: Abingdon.

Schlauch, Chris. 1990. Empathy as the Essence of Pastoral Psychotherapy. *Journal of Pastoral Care* 44: 3–17.

Schlauch, Chris. 1995. *Faithful Companioning: How Pastoral Counseling Heals.* Minneapolis: Fortress.

Scott, A. O. 2004. Jesus as a Box-Office Superhero. *New York Times,* March 7, 2004, Arts and Leisure: 21.

Shelp, Earl E., and Ronald H. Sunderland. 2000. *Sustaining Presence: A Model of Caring by People of Faith.* Nashville: Abingdon.

Stone, Howard W., and James O. Duke. 1996. *How to Think Theologically.* Minneapolis: Fortress.

Stuart, Elizabeth, and Adrian Thatcher. 1997. *People of Passion: What the Churches Teach about Sex.* London: Mowbray.

Taylor, Charles. 1992. *Multiculturalism and "The Politics of Recognition."* Princeton, NJ: Princeton University Press. Reprinted in David Theo Goldberg, ed., *Multiculturalism: A Critical Reader,* 75–106. Cambridge, MA: Blackwell, 1994.

The Book of Discipline. 2000. United Methodist Publishing House.

Thistlethwaite, Susan Brooks, and Mary Potter Engel, eds. 1990. *Lift Every Voice: Constructing Christian Theologies from the Underside.* San Francisco: Harper & Row.

Van Katwyk, Peter. 1993. A Family Observed: Theological and Family Systems Perspectives on the Grief Experience. *Journal of Pastoral Care* 47: 141–47.

Walker, Lenore. 1979. *The Battered Woman.* San Francisco: Harper & Row.

Weaver, Andrew J., Laura T. Flannelly, and John D. Preston. 2003. *Counseling Survivors of Traumatic Events: A Handbook for Pastors and Other Helping Professionals.* Nashville: Abingdon.

Index of Names and Subjects